THIRTEEN
AGAINST
THE BANK

THIRTEEN
AGAINST
THE BANK

•

by Norman Leigh

WILLIAM MORROW AND COMPANY, INC.
New York   1976

Printed in the United States of America.

1 2 3 4 5   80 79 78 77 76

Library of Congress Cataloging in Publication Data

Leigh, Norman.
    Thirteen against the bank.

    1. Gambling—London. 2. Gambling—Nice. 3. Roulette. I. Title.
HV6722.G86L65   795'.2   75-28280
ISBN 0-688-03004-1

This book is dedicated to Dianne Roberts, a great lady who stood by me in my hour of need, and to the twelve gallant and courageous men and women without whom this book would not have been possible.

foreword

This book is a true and detailed account of how a lifelong obsession led me to achieve what all expert opinion holds to be impossible—beating the table at roulette. I have changed certain names and places to protect the innocent —and the guilty. I fully expect a great deal of hostility, both from "experts" and from an industry which needs no lessons in ruthlessness, as you can judge for yourself from what happened in casinos in London and France to the group of law-abiding English people I brought together to "break the bank." Our only crime—to win methodically and consistently at roulette.

If I have found the perfect system for beating the wheel, why should I wish to reveal it to the whole world? Why am I not seated even now at the table before a vast pile of chips and plaques, turning myself into a millionaire? You will understand the answer to the question when you have read this book. Let me make it clear—my system is not a secret formula for winning easy money, far from it. It is damned hard money.

The events described here took place in 1966. Why have I waited so long to write about them? Simply because it did not occur to me until one evening in a hotel

bar in Hampshire when I was describing my roulette adventure to a friend, Derek Solity, a jewellery representative. He said it would make a marvellous book. The more I thought about it the more I had to agree. But even then I hesitated. There is a dark side to the mythology of casinos, strange stories of disappearances and the like, death and rumours of death. After all, the gambling industry is not run on the same lines as the Church of England and has vast profits to protect.

Inevitably, attempts will be made to discredit both my system and my character. Certainly I am no candidate for canonization. I have served a term of imprisonment because of incidents totally unconnected with roulette. Some two years after my return from Nice I set up a property consultancy in Twickenham and subsequently became involved in an alleged fraud case, for which I was sent to prison. This in turn merged into a criminal libel prosecution regarding material I published concerning a policeman. Rightly or wrongly, I elected to defend myself at the Old Bailey rather than be represented by counsel. I received an acquittal on the major charge but was convicted on a count of what amounted to publishing matter which could have resulted in a breach of the peace. For this I was sentenced to a subsequent term of imprisonment. Let me make one obvious point—one would not expect to find a lifelong obsession with gaming at a professional level in a lay preacher. To some extent my compulsion to make roulette history has been a jagged reef on which my life several times came near to foundering.

While a certain sleight-of-hand has been used to dramatize events, I should stress that real names have been changed to protect the members of my team. In getting cash out of France we committed an offense against that country's currency laws, and as members of

an organized syndicate they would have had tax problems in Britain.

However, let me assure the reader—I am willing to accept, in advance, *any challenge whatsoever* to the feasibility of my method for winning large sums at roulette, which I call the Reverse Labouchère system.

I put myself at no risk—thirteen of us proved that my method works and we proved it at the table, with real money.

NORMAN LEIGH

Hants, 1975

CURRENCY EXCHANGE RATES

In 1966, when most of this story took place, the following currency exchange rates were in effect:

13.7 francs = 1 pound

4.9 francs = 1 dollar

1 pound = 2.8 dollars

1 shilling = 14 cents

£90 = $250 (staking capital at
the Regency Club, London)

2,600 francs = £190 ($525)—maximum stake at
Casino Municipale, Nice

Throughout the book, figures have been rounded off.

1

By 2 P.M. on that searingly hot September day on the Côte d'Azur, under the bluest of all blue skies, the thirteen of us had assembled at pavement tables outside the Café Massena.

"It seems that everybody is present and correct, Mr. Leigh," said Oliver Blake in his twenty-two-carat Etonian accent. "Is there anything you wish to say to us before battle commences?"

Despite the usual small talk about their respective journeys from London, I could see clear signs of tension on the faces of my little assortment of unmistakably English men and women. Diagonally across the square, only fifty yards away, was the dull ochre building which housed the Casino Municipale in Nice. In sixty minutes the *tourneurs* would spin the brass spokes of the roulette wheels to open the day's gaming, and we would be staking the first chips of our attempt to break the bank.

Around us local habituées of the café were deep in their never-ending games of dice. In front of us the pavement was thronged by the cosmopolitan crowd endemic to the south of France—Germans, Americans, Italians, Scandinavians, Arabs; the young and beautiful, the smart and the innocent. Few gave our little party a second

glance. We fitted no obvious category and had little in common except our Englishness. The youngest of us was twenty-six, the oldest sixty. Our clothes ranged from the ostentatiously correct to the downright dowdy. Our accents covered the social scale from Oliver Blake's clipped Etonian drawl to working-class London. We included an office clerk with acne, a wealthy businessman, a very glamorous housewife, a minor civil servant, a timid widow who had never travelled abroad before, and a Londoner whose passport described him, rather inaccurately, as a clerk.

If the cynical locals around us had been told that we proposed to take on the unlimited reserves of the casino with a capital of only £90 ($250) each they would undoubtedly have exploded into fits of Gallic laughter. Perhaps there were some members of the group who were having last-minute doubts as the minutes raced towards three o'clock. One or two had given up safe jobs to make this trip. One or two *needed* to win big money for personal reasons. But were the "experts" correct in saying that there never had been and never would be a perfect system for winning at roulette? Were we within smelling distance of a tax-free fortune—or prime candidates for all the ignominies heaped on those broken by the wheel?

As far as I was concerned I had no fears. In a London gambling club, we had already proved that my method could work, proved it so successfully that every dirty, intimidatory trick in the book had been used to frighten us off. No, my own apprehensions at that moment were of a more serious nature.

Finishing my black coffee, I looked round the twelve faces and smiled.

"Well, ladies and gentlemen, three o'clock looms closer. I won't wish you luck, because luck has no place

in what we are about to do. Are there any final questions, no matter how trivial?"

"If any of them casino blokes speaks to me in French I'll be struggling to keep my end up, won't I?" said Keith Robinson, a small, wiry man with ginger hair, a Londoner from Shepherd's Bush.

"Perhaps Mrs. Richardson would act as interpreter if I'm not in sight," I said. Emma Richardson was in her middle thirties, on the small side, with ash-blond hair and extremely alert blue eyes. I knew little about her background at that point. Although I had gone out of my way to find sober, reliable people for this team, there were several whose specific backgrounds were something of a mystery. Being English is supposed to preclude any vulgar tendency to nosiness but it was not good manners that had stopped me prying too deeply into their domestic circumstances. The simple fact was that I did not give a damn.

My only interest in these people lay in their ability to play roulette six hours a day, strictly to my instructions. The "clerk," I had just discovered, was a professional criminal travelling on a false passport. But like the rest he had survived a long and difficult series of hurdles to be part of this final group of twelve, and that was all that mattered to me.

"I'll be happy to act as interpreter, but what exactly should we do if we're questioned by the staff?" asked Mrs. Richardson.

"Have as many witnesses present as possible if the management try to question you," I said. "Then produce your notepad and pen and ask for the questions to be put in writing. That always makes petty officials think twice—and you have a permanent record of what was asked."

"And what chips are we to buy at the outset, Mr. Leigh?" Blake asked.

It's hard with his type of Englishman, with a public-school background, to tell whether the excessive formality is a form of self-mockery. Blake was not without wit, but not everybody recognized it, and his mannered personality was to cause strain in the group. I knew already, for instance, that Mrs. Richardson detested him. He was a portly young man, only thirty-two but extremely stout, black hair brushed severely back from a pale, podgy face. He had very definite ideas of how an Englishman should decently comport himself—no matter what the temperature or the surroundings, none of us had ever seen him dressed in anything other than a heavy blue pinstripe suit and waistcoat. We shared some hairy moments, but never once did he address me as anything but Mr. Leigh. I presumed that like myself he had more complicated reasons for joining a roulette syndicate than the mere winning of tax-free money.

"This time I want you to put all your ninety pounds' staking capital into chips before you start," I said. "You won't lose anything like that in one shift, but it's better to have too many chips than to have to break off to buy more in the event of something going wrong."

"We can just carry them about with us like cash," Robinson said.

"No! It's illegal to be in possession of chips outside the casino. You must cash them in at the end of each shift." I explained that each person should put a third of his £90 in the red 2-franc chips, a third in the pink 5-franc chips and the rest in blue 10-franc chips. "When your stakes shoot up in a progression," I continued, "the table will pay you in high-denomination plaques rather than waste time shoving across vast piles of chips. The plaques here go from twenty-five francs to a thousand."

It was 2:30 P.M. One or two of the group signalled to the waiters. Apart from Hopplewell, who ordered his habitual large brandy, the others stuck to coffee or ice-cream. Hopplewell was sixty, some kind of company promoter in London, a morose and taciturn man whose livid drinker's face frequently took on a bluish tinge. In principle I would have preferred total abstinence, but I was not running a Boy Scout troop and if brandy or rum was vital to his performance at the table he was welcome to guzzle all day.

"Don't you blokes feel the heat with them suits on?" asked Keith Robinson, fanning his face. Knowing that Blake hated personal conversations which might come dangerously near to intimacy, I steered Robinson's mockery onto myself.

"I always wear these same clothes," I said. "It's my uniform—dark suit, white shirt, polka-dot bow tie, black shoes. Would any of you have trusted me to take you to a foreign country to play for high stakes if I'd been wearing jeans and a sweater?"

"What difference does clothes make?" he retorted.

"It's amazing what confidence a good suit inspires in people—getting into a hotel, parking a car. In a capitalist society it's up to each individual what price he puts on himself."

"This jacket cost twenty quid," he said indignantly, fingering his light grey, mass-produced sports coat.

"That isn't quite what I meant," I said tactfully.

"One thing you've never actually told us, Mr. Leigh," said Mrs. Richardson. "Why have you always insisted we come to this particular casino in this particular town?"

"It's as good as any other and I like Nice."

"You've been here lots of times, have you?"

"Once or twice. Just a little quirk, I suppose."

It was 2:45 P.M. We paid our *additions* and moved off

slowly across the square towards the casino building. Falling in step beside me at the rear of the group, Blake remarked in a gloomy voice: "God knows what's going to come of all this, Mr. Leigh."

With some hesitation we entered the outwardly shabby building and started up the staircase with the wrought-iron balustrade and dingy red carpet. As we reached the first-floor landing, where a chipped plaque bearing the legend "Casino Municipale" hung above the swing doors, the group seemed to hesitate. How could they succeed where so many thousands had failed? Wasn't the whole mythology of French gaming riddled with death and disaster?

"When we go through that door, at no time must we show the slightest sign of our being an organized group," I said, merely intending to be practical but no doubt adding to their unspoken doubts.

Blake saved the moment. Turning to face the others, he said, rather theatrically: "Come, come, one does not make history by standing in the shadows biting one's nails."

A few of them smiled. Not for the first time I congratulated myself on having picked him as my Number Two.

There was nothing furtive or secretive about our entrance. On the contrary, I wasted no time in going with Blake in search of the *Chef de Casino*—the director of the establishment—while those who had arrived late from London the previous evening produced their passports at the desk to obtain admission cards.

As play had not yet started, the Chef de Casino was standing only a few feet inside the enormous gaming salon, a stocky, balding man in white tie and tails. I did not need to ask any of the staff to point him out. As we

approached he gave us one of the warm smiles he reserved specially for welcoming the new day's quota of lambs for the shearing.

"Good afternoon, Monsieur le Chef," I began.

"Good afternoon, messieurs," he replied courteously. His English was very good, and so, too, was his German, Italian and Spanish, probably even his Arabic. For a man in his position, linguistic versatility was one of the tools of the trade.

"Monsieur," I said, "this gentleman and I and a few friends feel we have a system which can beat the casino. Before we commence playing, do we have your assurance that there will be no objection to our playing this system?"

A look of boredom flickered across his broad, shiny face. We gave the appearance of men who knew the world—Blake was almost exactly the Frenchman's idea of an English milord—yet here we were, not only planning our own ruin but naively giving public notice of our intentions. Naturally he believed, as does the whole gaming world, that no system ever devised could defeat the limitless resources of a casino. A few individuals have had fluke successes over the years, like the man in the song who "broke the bank at Monte Carlo," but they are no serious threat. The casino has merely to keep the wheels turning and wait—the bank always wins in the end.

He bestowed upon us another of his warm, professional smiles. "But messieurs, we positively *welcome* all system players. You have my assurance—no obstacle will be put in your way."

"Thank you, Monsieur le Chef."

"It is my pleasure, messieurs."

We crossed the room to the roulette tables.

"Was it wise to put him on the alert?" asked Blake.

"Once we start winning he'll know we're a team anyway. No, I just wanted him to give us his approval. That will make it harder for him if he wants to throw us out. Nobody can reproach us for not being completely above board."

"He certainly seemed a civil enough chap."

"One of the finest—until you're cleaned out. Then he has a slightly irritating habit of laughing in your face."

"You do know him, then?" said Blake curiously.

"Yes."

"Well, he has given us his word—"

"We'll see. Not all nationalities share this quaint English belief that a man's word is sacred, you know."

"It's their loss, I would say."

Shown every politeness due to those about to feel the chill wind, our first shift of six took seats at the table which had the lowest minimum stake. They were to cover the table's six even chances from 3 P.M. until 9 P.M., when our second shift of six would take over until close of play at 3 A.M. The even-chance bets in roulette are red or black; odd or even; high or low. When the player wins a bet on one of these, the bank pays even money—the amount of the bet.

The fact that six English people had suddenly commenced staking the same amount on all the even chances caused some raised eyebrows among the other players but as the salon began to fill up, the activities of our first shift soon became submerged in the general flow of the casino. For the first two or three hours nothing much happened: that is, there were no spectacular gains or losses. Our six players merely placed their chips and worked out their next stakes on their notepads.

My role was that of nonplaying captain and permanent reserve. As I moved round the table behind them, watching for any signs of difficulty with the unaccustomed

French chips and plaques, I noticed how little the place had changed down the years. Under the chandeliers, the patrons could almost have been taking part in a silent film, especially those elderly local residents who came there each day to reflect on the long-lost glories of more warm-blooded times. For me that afternoon, the huge salon with its marble pillars and faded plush seemed haunted by the ghosts of my own past. Any casino is purely and simply an efficient trap for parting customers from their money, but this particular trap had taken up a major part of my life.

"Not at all what I imagined," observed Oliver Blake when I joined him briefly at the bar. He eyed me curiously. "There are better places, aren't there?"

I had no desire to explain to him my obsession with roulette and with this casino in particular. I was sure a man of his standing would not understand, even if I understood myself. On the other hand I did not want him worrying that I might have something to hide—our sole business here was to play method roulette with as few distractions as possible.

I said casually: "I came here once with my father a few years ago. We lost quite a bit, at least by our standards. I think that's why I've always thought it would be nice to have a success here if one was going to have a success at all."

It was around 6 P.M. on that first day when Mrs. Heppenstall, a rather timid little widow from the seaside town of Hastings, ran into a favourable progression on her particular chance, *pair* (the even numbers). The basis of my system, the Reverse Labouchère, was to maximize one's winnings during a favourable run and to end quickly a losing sequence, the cunning part being that when the stakes rise during a winning run the player risks the bank's money, that is, money he or she

has already won. I will explain later in detail how I evolved the system and how it works.

Within half an hour of the start of her progression Mrs. Heppenstall was in a sequence where *pair* (even) predominated over *impair* (odd) by roughly 3 to 1. Adhering faithfully to the staking pattern, she began to accumulate a loose pyramid of chips and plaques.

Blake and I stood behind her, ready to help with her paperwork if she showed signs of faltering. With approximately thirty spins to the hour on a French table she had on average only a minute to calculate her next stake and then select chips and plaques to the exact amount. She was too busy with her calculations to sort out her winnings so I moved beside her chair and put her plaques and chips into neat denominational piles so that she could easily see what to pick for each bet.

It was as well that I was within reach in my role of nonplaying captain. Throughout their training period I had warned the team against the three greatest dangers a method-roulette player faces—drink, women and conversation. The slightest interference can upset the concentration of a method player and produce a mental blockage. Obviously drink and women were not serious contenders for the attention of the fifty-four-year-old widow from Hastings, but sure enough, just as she was working out a stake in the order of 1,500 francs (roughly £110 at over 13 francs to the pound—about $300 at almost 5 francs to the dollar) another woman player leaned over intrusively.

"Do tell me, *please*—what system are you using?" she asked.

I had a drill to cover such situations. Whipping out my own notebook, I quickly wrote on a blank page: DO NOT ENTER INTO CONVERSATION WITH THAT WOMAN!

I tore the sheet out and placed it on the green baize

in front of Mrs. Heppenstall. Without the slightest sign of a fluff, she selected a handful of plaques and chips.

It was then that the team first experienced the weirdest phenomenon in gaming, one of the eeriest sounds I know.

The table staff began to clap their hands, a quietly insistent handclapping just loud enough to be audible throughout the enormous salon. They clapped to a slow, rhythmic code.

"What are they doing?" Blake whispered urgently.

"It's a language they have for passing messages," I replied. "I don't know the whole code, but at the moment they're spreading the word that someone is winning heavily."

Within seconds, casino officials began to arrive at the table to watch Mrs. Heppenstall as she went on winning and increasing her stakes. A few minutes later the Chef de Casino himself appeared.

"Look at them," Blake said in astonishment. "Their eyes are positively *willing* the ball to drop into an odd number!"

Mrs. Heppenstall's progression was our very first, and by casino standards her gains were not significant—but there they were, from the director downwards, summoning up all the psychic powers at their disposal to govern the destination of that small ivory ball.

They did not succeed in altering the pattern being thrown up by the wheel. For another hour Mrs. Heppenstall went on winning roughly three times to each time she lost. Under my method she would have stopped escalating her stakes and returned to a completely new sequence of bets starting with a mere 5 francs when she reached the 2,600-franc maximum. She never got that far. As she was selecting plaques and chips for a stake of around £170 ($475) the *Chef de Partie*, who supervises

play at the table and adjudicates in case of dispute, announced that no more bets could be taken until fresh reserves of capital had been brought up from the bank. The table had run out of chips.

Mrs. Heppenstall had broken it!

The casino officials stared at her with a mixture of curiosity and bewilderment. Other players craned and jostled to get a look at her notepad.

Seeing that Mrs. Heppenstall was clearly embarrassed by all this attention, I leaned forward to congratulate her. One of these protracted winning progressions—"mushrooms" as we called them—can be a terrifying ordeal for a shy person. There is no harsher spotlight than that directed on a roulette player who seems to have found the magic formula.

"I can't believe it," she said, shaking her head at the heaps of plastic discs and rectangles spread before her on the green baize.

"I should put the large-denomination stuff into your handbag," I told her. I saw the Chef de Casino coming round the table.

"*Vos amis jouent un système très formidable, n'est-ce-pas, Monsieur Leigh?*" he said, producing one of his selection of smiles. The fact that he spoke in French was a sure sign that he was annoyed, a trait of his I'd noticed down the years. He left, giving a slight bow.

I turned to Blake. "He says we're playing a formidable system."

"It's a bit early for him to be getting shirty with us," Blake said. "All this panic over a few thousand francs? I should have thought they'd be big enough to take it in their stride."

"Obviously if somebody starts winning with a system they want to know what the system is. That's their job. Don't worry. It's early days yet."

Blake's uneasiness stemmed from his aversion to any form of public scandal or notoriety. My main concern, which I didn't communicate to him, was how many more such wins we could have before the casino authorities decided to eliminate the danger of our group breaking the bank in the grand manner, and in what way they would go about it. Suicides, deaths and mysterious disappearances are major themes in the shadowy history of French casinos, much of it rumour perhaps but nonetheless disquieting for that.

Naturally I kept these thoughts from the rest of the group, most of whom had known absolutely nothing about roulette until they had met me. Hints of how ruthless French casinos can be would only upset their concentration.

At 9 P.M., our second shift of six gathered at the table, each standing behind the chair of the player whose allocated chance he was taking over. As the first six rose from their seats, leaving their notepads and loose chips on the table, the second six quickly took their places. This was another key factor in my planning—a straight session of six hours' nonstop roulette is arduous enough, both mentally and physically, without having to do it on your feet. There are usually only nine or ten chairs at a French roulette table, with possibly forty people standing. We had learned in London to forget all considerations of etiquette: those seats *had* to be ours.

Having seen the second shift of six taking up the staking progressions of those they had replaced, I was preparing to go with Mrs. Heppenstall to the cash desk to pay in her winnings when Emma Richardson asked if she might have a word with me. I asked Mr. Milton to go with Mrs. Heppenstall and then give the cash to Blake. Mrs. Richardson and I went to the bar.

"I wanted to tell you this morning, but I didn't know

where you were staying and I was pretty sure you wouldn't want the others to know," she said, lighting a cigarette. "Guess who was in my compartment in the train from Victoria."

"Who?"

"No sooner was I in my compartment when a tall and quite distinguished-looking man took the seat opposite. He was reading *Le Figaro* but when the train started he asked me in good English if I would watch his luggage for a few minutes. When he came back we started chatting. He said he was returning to the south of France after a business trip to London. Mr. Leigh"—she took hold of my arm, urgently—"can you imagine my surprise when he told me he was a senior officer in the Police des Jeux, attached to their headquarters in this very town?"

"Are you sure he said Police des Jeux?" I asked, without undue excitement.

"Oh yes—he even showed me his warrant card. Quite a coincidence, I thought." She sipped her martini, waiting for my reaction. The Police des Jeux is the section of the French legal system responsible for the municipal casinos.

"What else did he say?" I asked.

"Only that he'd been to Scotland Yard for a conference. Oh yes—and he invited me to a cocktail party tonight. Should I go?"

Our group had caused a stir in one of London's better known casinos. Our own police were satisfied I was not using the roulette group as a front for smuggling or currency evasion (I knew this because the detective they had infiltrated had resigned from his job to come with this group and was playing at that very moment at our table!). Yet, legal or not, our intentions were obviously of interest to the French authorities, even though it

appeared from my earlier conversation with the Chef de Casino that he had not been warned about us in advance.

"Yes, go to the party," I said. "No harm in that. Play it by ear. Don't say anything about the group—and don't tell anybody else. Perhaps you'll find out if they're aware of our existence."

"Not even tell *Mister* Blake?"

"He'd only worry unnecessarily. You know what he's like."

"Stuck-up pompous prig. I know bloody well what he's like. I—"

"Look, Emma, I don't care how much some of you may loathe and detest each other privately but I'd be very angry if silly personal animosities ruined this team's chances. We can only work this thing with multiples of six players—one drops out now and the whole thing collapses."

"I'll keep it bottled up in future, don't worry."

She went off to dinner with those of the first shift who were too hungry or tired to stay and watch how the second six fared. At 10:30 P.M. the casino was at its busiest, the elderly relics having retired to bed to dream of grander days, making way for the greedy, curious and brainless of all nationalities, when Hopplewell hit a progression on black. Even with a predominance of only minimally above 2 to 1 in his favour, he quickly reached the table limit on his staking pattern, which by the rules of our system meant he must immediately revert to the smallest stakes.

Hopplewell had won 29,000 francs (£2100—$5,900). Mrs. Heppenstall's win had been much larger, 49,000 francs—she had had a much longer winning progression —which was why the table had found itself without enough capital.

When Blake, our treasurer, finished cashing up at 3 A.M. he invited those of the group still in the casino to come back to what he referred to as his "pub" for a drink. We went by car and taxi and found that by *pub* he meant one of the town's better hotels. (The use of the word *pub* for any hotel, be it Claridge's in London or the George V in Paris, was his only concession to slang.) When we went upstairs we discovered that he was occupying a substantial suite, which at Riviera prices cannot have been cheap.

It was extremely hot, perhaps 95 degrees, even at four in the morning. Outside in the gardens cicadas were chirruping in the thousands. On the dining table Blake began to lay out thin wads of French currency. The cash desk had paid out mainly in large denominations, brownish 500-franc notes showing the head of Pascal, and multicoloured 100-franc notes depicting Cardinal Richelieu in his skullcap.

There was, however, enough of the smaller stuff to make a substantial spread of money. For several moments nobody spoke.

"I make it seventy-eight thousand francs," Blake said.

"What's that in real money?" asked Keith Robinson.

"At about thirteen point seven francs to the pound—five thousand seven hundred pounds, give or take a franc or two [$15,900]."

"Almost six grand, first day out? Must be encouraging," Robinson commented, pretending to faint by collapsing backwards onto the large sofa. Nobody laughed.

"As agreed, we will share out our winnings every day," Blake said. "Arrangements have been made through my own bank in London with a bank here if anyone wishes to avail themselves of that facility."

"Oh, I wouldn't trust no foreign banks," Robinson said. "Give us the cash, Oliver."

And so Blake divided up those thin, crisp wads of French currency. He and I were each taking 10 percent of the total winnings, which gave us 7,800 francs each (£570–$1,590) and the other eleven divided the remainder equally, which gave them about 5,600 francs each (£410–$1,150).

Blake had brought a supply of his favourite white envelopes from London and into these he put shares for those who had preferred to go to bed.

"I've got to let my wife have some of this straight-away," said Terry Baker. "What's the situation about getting money out of this country?"

"There's a government limit, but all you have to do is post it home by ordinary mail," I said. "Put each big note in a separate envelope so that if there is an interception you won't lose too much. Fold the note in a sheet of paper and use a different postbox for each envelope. Naturally you don't put your name or address here on it."

"But that's illegal," exclaimed the gloomy Mr. Fredericks. "You've always been most careful to warn us not to do *anything* illegal."

"There's no way of tracing who sent the notes if they're intercepted," I said patiently. "What's more, we wouldn't be breaking our own laws. You do want to send your winnings home and have something to show for this, don't you?"

"Yes, of course."

"Right then. We're not taking much of a risk."

When the others had gone, and Blake and I were left alone, he said: "One sometimes envies the ease with which other nationalities express their feelings. At a time like this, one almost feels like shouting 'Whoopee' and throwing one's arms about."

"Please do, I won't mind."

"What a ludicrous thought. Come on, I'll drive you back."

Driving through the dark, deserted streets, he finally allowed himself the indulgence of a verbal arm-fling. "Mr. Leigh, one sees the occasional drama as a stockbroker, but I'm *bloody* sure that never before has a scheme of this magnitude been launched by a single individual. It astounds me, frankly. If somebody had told me a year ago this would be happening to me now I would have called him a liar to his face."

"Let's see how things work out."

He stopped the red Sunbeam Alpine outside my hotel. I was exhausted. As I made to open the car door he said: "One hesitates to pry, of course, but it all seems too amazing. Where did you get the idea in the first place?"

"From an old book actually. I must show it to you sometime. Good night."

Blake drove off back to his palatial apartments while I climbed the stairs of my second-class hotel to my modest, ten-pound-a-day room.

It was stiflingly hot, and the din of the insects together with my own overtiredness kept me awake. I got out of bed, poured myself a large whisky and drank it in the dark, sitting on the edge of the bed.

Before the sudden arrival of the Mediterranean dawn I had finished the bottle, fighting off a black mood of loneliness and doubt. How often in the past fifteen years had my obsession with beating the casino brought me this far, right to the brink of success, only to suffer defeat and humiliation? How could I explain to an upper-class Englishman like Blake the compulsion that had ruled most of my adult life, when even to me it remained an enigma.

2

My obsession with roulette is easier to trace than to explain. I was born in 1928 in the City of London, where my father was a pub licensee. Subsequently he moved south of the Thames to Peckham Rye, where he had a pub called the Queen, and later to Hertford Heath, where he had the Townshend Arms. We were always fairly well off. At school I was naturally fluent at languages but extremely bad at math. I had no liking for any organized sport, not because I was a weedy boy but simply because I rejected any idea that the individual should be made to succumb to the majority view.

Reading was my passion during the teen-age years, especially history. The barren, austere life of wartime Britain could be forgotten in the novels of Alexandre Dumas. I developed a strong fantasy identification with a type of hero best described as the *grand seigneur*. Sir Percy Blakeney, the Scarlet Pimpernel, was my idol when other boys were collecting photographs of football players and film stars.

In those days I read everything in sight including, at one desperate stage, an old *Chambers' Encyclopedia* published in 1896. I read it like a novel, from cover to cover. For some reason I found myself studying the entry under

roulette until I had practically memorized it.

Basically roulette is a banking game—the individual bets his money against the bank's money. The equipment consists of a wheel and a cloth layout, usually green. Each compartment of this layout signifies a different form of bet.

		0			
PASSE (19-36)		1	2	3	**MANQUE** (1-18)
		4	5	6	
		7	8	9	
		10	11	12	
PAIR (even)		13	14	15	**IMPAIR** (odd)
		16	17	18	
		19	20	21	
		22	23	24	
NOIR (black)		25	26	27	**ROUGE** (red)
		28	29	30	
		31	32	33	
		34	35	36	

Instead of cash it is normal throughout the world to use chips of different shapes and colours to represent various amounts of money. The odds vary. The bank will pay from 35 to 1 if you bet on one particular number, down to even money—the amount of your bet—if you bet on any of the six outside compartments: red (*rouge*), or black (*noir*); odd (*impair*), or even (*pair*); high (*passe*), the numbers between nineteen and thirty-six, or low (*manque*), the numbers between one and eighteen.

The French wheel has thirty-seven compartments, one for each number up to thirty-six and one for zero. Half

the numbered slots are red, the rest black. The game starts when the *tourneur,* the croupier who turns the wheel, calls, *"Faites vos jeux"* (Make your bets), and spins the wheel in one direction while throwing in the ball in the opposite direction. As the ball begins to slow down the tourneur calls, *"Rien ne va plus"* (The betting is closed). When the ball stops he announces the winning number and whether it is red or black, odd or even, high or low.

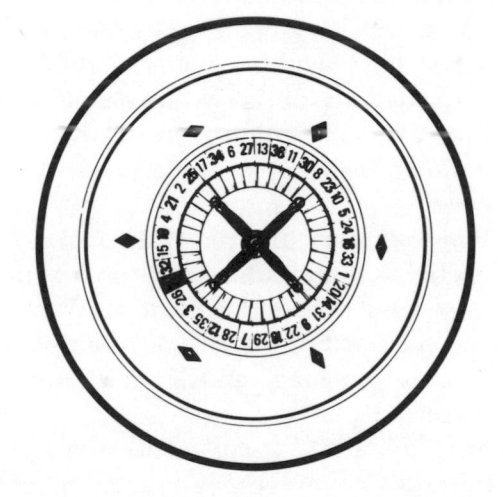

Another croupier drags in the losing chips with his stick (or rake) and pushes out the winnings. There are many ways of betting, on groups or lines of numbers, but the bank always has an advantage in that it wins all bets when the ball ends up in the zero compartment. (Not quite *all* bets, for you can stake on zero.)

One thing puzzled me, right from the start. "Nobody has ever yet succeeded in making a profit out of the game of roulette," said the encyclopedia, although the advantage to the bank from zero was only 1.4 percent on even chances.

It is possible I had heard my father talking about roulette. Nevertheless, of all the dreary stuff one is exposed to in reading encyclopedias for relaxation why was it I stored that fact away?

When I left school my father assumed I would join him in the hotel business, but I associated that with a certain subservience. Having no real interest in any other career, I became a printing apprentice. Then, under the government's powers to direct labour, I was sent to be an apprentice aviation electrician at Broxbourne in Hertfordshire. I was, strangely enough, quite happy about this. I have always liked working under a duly constituted authority—provided its decisions are manifestly fair. To know exactly what the rules are and then to triumph *without breaking* authority's own code—that is my idea of a challenge.

I was then called up into the army, which decided to use my electrical qualifications by giving me clerical duties in prisoner-of-war camps, first at Wookey Hall in Somerset and then at Oxford, where I became a German interpreter after teaching myself that language from gramophone records.

On leaving the army, I worked for the Hertfordshire War Agricultural Committee as a branch petroleum manager, touring the district in my official car checking petrol station stocks with a dipstick to ensure that nobody was cheating. The war was over, but the restrictions remained, to the profit of the crooked.

It was at this time that my father took me on several trips to the casinos of France. He suffered from a conviction that he could win at roulette with the Martingale system. A look at the Martingale may help you understand how I finally devised my own method. The idea of this method is to double up your bet after each loss, until you have recouped your total losses. Unrestricted

doubling up being the quickest road to ruin known to man, you must also set a limit to the number of times you will chase your losses. Let us take three losing bets as our limit.

Imagine you are staking units of £1 on black. On the first spin red comes up, and you lose. Your next bet is, therefore, £2. You lose again; so your third bet is £4. If this also loses, you revert to a bet of £1, having lost a total of £7.

If, however, your first bet had won, you would have taken back your £1 stake plus the £1 the bank paid. Your next bet would again have been £1 on black. You would have carried on with bets of £1 until the next time you lost. In theory the Martingale should show a profit of one unit for every spin of the wheel, and it is, of course, a remarkably simple system to operate.

In practice it put my father in a constant war of attrition with the wheel. The insidious attraction of the Martingale is that it produces small but consistent winnings and also seems such an easy way of recovering losses. In fact the wins are never big enough to compensate for the amounts you lose when the wheel turns against you. The table has almost unlimited capital and can stand long sequences when the player is winning on even-chance bets; the player cannot sustain equally long sequences when he is doubling up and losing. The law of averages says that red and black will even out eventually, but following the law of averages to infinity is not for mortals.

We went to casinos in Deauville, Trouville, Nice and other French towns and invariably we had to come home sooner than we had planned because our money had run out. Fair enough. One goes into a gaming salon perfectly well aware that it is a jungle where welfare-state safety nets do not exist. That is the main attraction of gambling,

the exposure to genuine drama. You win or you lose, and your character is put to the test in both eventualities. My father and I could never have won consistently, because we treated the whole thing too casually. This is typical of most players, even those who think they are working methodically. Still, our losses were hardly ruinous, a few hundred pounds at most.

An experience we had one summer in the late fifties was to have a lasting effect on me. It was in the same Casino Municipale in Nice to which I brought my party of twelve to play the Reverse Labouchère ten years later. Having played for three days, my father ran into an adverse sequence of some magnitude. Doubling up to recoup his losses, he came to the end of all our money, about three hundred pounds, not only our roulette capital but the rest of our subsistence allowance too.

"I'm getting up now," he said to the table staff. The Chef de Casino was beside the table, as always taking a friendly interest in regular patrons who were losing.

"But why, monsieur?" he asked. He was younger then, with a few more strands of hair, but little else that would change over the years.

"I've run out of money," my father said, matter-of-factly.

The Chef de Casino laughed. A short laugh, neither malicious nor particularly triumphant. A short laugh, that was all, in our faces.

We walked to the British Consulate to apply for financial assistance. There is no need to tell anyone who has had the misfortune to require help from a consulate how degrading it is to ask to borrow money after losing at roulette.

"Leigh, put out that cigarette," snapped a snotty young underling to my father as we stood before his desk. I would have reacted, but my father frowned at

me to keep quiet. This pipsqueak then demanded to know why we had no money.

"We lost it," I said, knowing that any mention of the casino would be a mistake.

"How do you mean, *lost* it?" he asked contemptuously.

"We can't find it," I replied. "It may have been stolen or it may just have dropped out of our pockets."

Grudgingly it was decided we were entitled to help. They took our passports as security and gave us temporary travel documents and distress warrants for the rail fare, a matter of fourteen pounds each. They also paid our hotel bill. These were loans, of course.

My father is an extremely conventional man, staid, determinedly respectable, yet if this incident caused him any embarrassment or humiliation he did not show it. He never again referred to it.

That particular episode made me more interested in the actual mathematics of roulette. It seemed puzzling that nobody was supposed to be able to win at it when the odds in the bank's favour were only 1.4 percent on even-chance bets, a slight advantage that comes from the zero slot on the wheel. If you bet on a single number or combination of numbers and the ball drops into zero, the bank wins. On the six even-chance bets, if the ball drops into zero, the table either takes half of your stake (*partager*) or you can leave your chips (*en prison*—imprisoned) until the next spin. If you win on the next spin, you get the whole stake back, but the bank does not pay you. If you lose on the next spin, you lose the lot. This option reduces the average amount the bank wins in the case of even-chance bets and didn't seem reason enough to me for the apparent fact that the bank always wins.

Whether I would have taken my interest in the theory of roulette any further than idle scribbling on bits of

paper but for a coincidence is hard to say. At least it seemed like a coincidence at the time—now I can see it as one more link in a pattern, for I have no doubt I was fated to spend much of my life trying to find a way to beat the wheel.

When my parents moved to the south coast to take over a New Forest hotel near the Hampshire village of New Milton I went with them and took a job as a clerk with a local firm of builders' merchants. Like so many people who have a vague idea they are destined for some special role in life, generally with little justification, I was content to drift from day to day in humdrum jobs, waiting for The Sign that would tell me where my life was destined to lead.

I met Walter Green one sunny day in his builder's yard in the village of Ashley. He was one of our customers, and there was a dispute over a load of cement. For some reason the subject of Grace Kelly's marriage to Prince Rainier of Monaco came up during our argument about the cement. That took us to gambling, via Monte Carlo, and then to his claim that he thought he had found a way of winning at roulette.

We spent the whole afternoon standing among those bags of cement in his yard, excitedly telling each other what we knew about Martingales, *paroles, montants* and *demontants,* all the elaborate numerical rituals roulette players have devised to achieve the impossible. He was the very first person with whom I had been able to discuss the theory of roulette, and when he asked me to his flat in Bournemouth that night to show me his system I jumped at the chance.

When I arrived at his place that evening it was not, however, to learn much about roulette but to fall immediately in love with the woman he was living with: Mary—elegant, forty years old, glorious auburn hair, sad

brown eyes in a pale face. The contrast between her and the coarse-mannered builder was well-nigh incredible, and I quickly developed romantic visions of myself gallantly rescuing her.

"Well now, old boy," said Walter Green, rubbing his hands together, "I suggest you and I get down to brass tacks—I've ordered a case of whisky from the off-license."

I had not misheard him. A case of whisky and soda siphons arrived shortly afterward. Two hours later we were garrulous and glowing. In the time it took him to make a phone call from another room, Mary and I decided we had a truly great passion for each other.

Drink, women and conversation—these defeat more roulette players than the laws of chance.

For two months I went almost every evening to Walter's flat in Holdenhurst Road, Bournemouth, where he had a toy roulette wheel and limitless supplies of graph paper. I did not know for some time that he had never actually seen a real table, having picked everything up from a book. Nor did I learn until later that his building company was almost bankrupt and that in his desperation he had decided a major gaming coup was his only hope of financial salvation. I might have been more skeptical if I had given our practice sessions all my concentration— Mary and I had developed such passion for each other that we could hardly wait for his incessant intake of whisky to put him under.

Despite all this, however, he did manage to show me the Fitzroy system. Like all the others it is a method of controlling both the amount you stake and also your chances of hitting a favourable sequence. Walter's variation should ideally have been played by eight people. It involved staking on colour combinations and using three columns to control the amounts won or lost.

Of course, his system did not *guarantee* that you

would win. No system does that. When the wheel runs against you it is implacable.

Despite Walter's fondness for whisky we completed tens of thousands of sequences on his toy wheel, and the results were impressive. We decided to find someone with five thousand pounds to invest in backing us. That was when Walter discovered that Mary and I were having an affair.

We broke up one beautiful August evening in the South Western Hotel, Bournemouth, where we were meeting to compose an advertisement that would intrigue potential backers.

As soon as Walter entered the lounge bar I sensed trouble. He was drunk and opened proceedings by shouting, "You filthy bastard."

In defense of my own irresponsible conduct I can only say that I had been shy with girls in adolescence and that early manhood had given me a powerful urge to make up for lost time. However, I learned something, the ease with which a great deal of hard work had been destroyed by mixing sex with roulette—and also that I must curb my own weakness for playing the *grand seigneur* role, that of the aristocrat who takes his pleasures where they come and does not give a damn for the consequences. The most important lesson I learnt from this —and was to go on learning—is the paradox that the people who are seriously attracted to the idea of casinos and gambling are the very last to be temperamentally capable of the single-minded dedication required to implement a system. Walter Green, like so many of the men I was subsequently forced to take on as partners, was not a real method player but a gambler. There is a fundamental difference. I think it was Dr. Johnson, fount of most English common sense, who summed it up when he said that a gambler resigns to chance those things that are best left to reason alone.

A gambler is always looking for a big win, a magic thrill. A method player concerns himself with percentages and the ultimate results of prolonged sequences.

This is one of the hardest parts of organizing a gaming syndicate. Few newspapers are willing to take advertisements connected with gambling, always suspecting a confidence trick, but on the staff of the local evening paper, the Bournemouth *Daily Echo,* happened to be a distant cousin of mine. He was willing to slip a small ad into the paper without putting it through the usual channels. A few days later the following appeared in the personal column of the classified section:

FRENCH RIVIERA. ACTIVE PARTNERSHIP AVAILABLE IN ENTERPRISE ON THE CÔTE D'AZUR. QUALIFICATION— £250. BOX . . .

I bought a toy wheel and waited for replies. There were a dozen or so. I made appointments to see them in the evening after work, fired not by any sense of destiny and not yet at the obsessional stage but merely hoping to make money.

At my first appointment, at a large house in Oxford Road, Bournemouth, I was shown into a sumptuous bedroom where reclined a petite but outstandingly beautiful blond girl wearing only a short blue housecoat and nylon panties. Standing at the end of the bed was a tall good-looking man smoking through a cigarette holder. He was easily six feet four inches in height, with dark curly hair and an aquiline nose. He was wearing a velvet smoking-jacket and, just in case the message wasn't clear enough, in one hand he held a silver-topped cane.

"I am Mrs. Mark Saunders," said the young woman. "Thank you very much for calling."

"My name is Norman Leigh," I replied. "I am looking for someone to provide the capital for a roulette system and to go to the south of France to play in a casino."

The tall man addressed me in a superior drawl.

"I am Mark Saunders. I deal in property here in Bournemouth and in Bristol. I merely answered your little advertisement from curiosity. Now you're here I suppose we might as well see if there's anything to it."

Ignoring the dismissive tone of his voice, I laid out the small wheel and some notepads on the bed, firmly refusing to let my eyes linger on the naked limbs of the unabashed Mrs. Saunders. For an hour she acted as tourneur while I demonstrated the Fitzroy method. The results were impressive. The haughty Mr. Saunders told me to leave my address. I was fairly certain I would never hear from him again.

My next call was to a substantial house in the wealthy Bournemouth suburb of Dean Park. There was a Bentley in the drive, and for a moment I thought of turning back. Mark Saunders had obviously dismissed me as a clerk with delusions of grandeur. Perhaps that's all I was. However, some kind of latent obstinacy made me go through with it. Feeling extremely embarrassed, I was shown into the lounge to meet Mr. Albert Dimmock, a substantial local bookmaker, flashy in dress and speech.

As soon as I said that long study had convinced me I had a method for winning at roulette he exploded. "What the bloody hell do you take me for—a steamer?" he snapped (*steamer* being underworld rhyming slang for a fool or sucker: steam-tug, mug).

"I'm sorry," I replied stiffly. "I was hoping you were an intelligent man and would give me a fair hearing."

"Listen, son," he growled, his face red with anger, "if you're on the con game you'd better get yourself a cleverer pitch than that. Do you think I look like a bloody mark?"

"If I were a confidence trickster do you think I'd see an intended victim in his own home?" I said weakly. He looked me up and down, shaking his head, obviously

· 40 ·

realizing that I was too naive to be a conman. I offered to demonstrate my method but he was not interested. He did, however, give me a fatherly lecture intended to frighten me off the idea of roulette systems for life.

"You don't know what dangerous waters you're dabbling in, son," he said. "Five years ago my nephew got some mad idea he'd found a winning system. *He* was going to clean up on the roulette tables at Monte Carlo. He wouldn't listen to anybody. He mortgaged and borrowed until he had a few thousand quid, then he raced down to Monte to make his pile. Poor bastard—lost the lot in a week. Came back here to Bournemouth too bloody ashamed even to go home. A few days later a hotel cleaner found him in his room with his brains spattered all over the bed. That's why I get so mad when I hear anybody talking about unbeatable systems. Do yourself a bit of good, son—forget it."

Ignoring this ominous warning, I went ahead with my appointments. Most people were quite polite. "Not quite our cup of tea" was the kind of phrase they used to brush me off. I don't think any of them regarded me as dishonest, for I always stressed the point that the £250 (about $700) I was asking them to invest on fares, expenses and staking money would always be in their possession, and that we would be working as genuine partners, myself standing to gain nothing unless my system worked, in which case I would take 50 percent of the profits. But if they didn't think I was crooked, they certainly classed me as insane—everybody has these fantasies, but only a madman would try to make them reality. Night after night I would return to my parents' home feeling utterly depressed and worthless. How could I, a young clerk in a cheap suit, convince anyone that I had found a way to beat the bank?

There was one name left on my list of replies to the

advertisement. More out of politeness than with any hope of finding a partner, I set off to call on him. The name was Harper-Biggs. The address turned out to be a large house in Westbourne, another of Bournemouth's moneyed districts. I was shown into an enormous lounge by the daily help. Mrs. Harper-Biggs, a tall, raw-boned woman, was sitting by the hearth of an open fireplace that lacked only an ox roasting on a spit. Knowing rejection was inevitable, I thought I might as well get it over with quickly and introduced myself without hesitation.

"My name is Norman Leigh. I'm looking for a partner in a gambling scheme."

Her long and rather fearsome face showed no reaction.

"Please take a seat, Mr. Leigh, and tell me what it's all about," she said.

Putting the small roulette wheel on the coffee table, I said, "I believe I have a system for winning at roulette and wish to find a partner who will put up the capital for us both to travel to the south of France and try my system on the tables at one of the municipal casinos. The sum required is two hundred and fifty pounds. Naturally I'm prepared to demonstrate the system on this toy wheel."

Without hesitation she said, "Very well then, get on with the demonstration."

Two hours later I stopped the wheel and waited for her to say something. She must have been in her middle forties then, an impassive yet strangely awkward-looking woman, not exactly thin but with such prominent bones that she looked positively gaunt; her clothes were expensively tailored yet there was always too much wrist showing and when she stood up the impression of awkwardness was even more pronounced, for she was easily six feet tall! Equally striking was her manner; nothing, it

seemed, could ever surprise her or, indeed, move her into any display of emotion whatsoever.

Still with the same long, sad face she said, "Well, Mr. Leigh, when do we start?"

Concealing my own excitement, I said there was a Channel steamer leaving Southampton for Le Havre the following Thursday.

"Yes, I agree," she said in her well-bred monotone. "As Shakespeare said, ' 'twere better 'twere done quickly.' " She stretched out a long arm and gave a couple of tugs on a cord hanging by the fireplace. A few seconds later a small man with horn-rimmed spectacles came deferentially into the room.

"Herbert, dear," said the expressionless voice, "this is Mr. Leigh. He and I have decided to travel down to Nice next Thursday. You remember I said his advertisement probably referred to some gambling scheme or another. Well, I've decided to take the bull by the horns. The capital Mr. Leigh needs is two hundred and fifty pounds."

"Very well, my dear," said Mr. Harper-Biggs, politely leaving the room. Amazed as I was that the staid, middle-aged wife of a Bournemouth bank inspector was coolly prepared to leave for France at a moment's notice on what was by any conventional standards a harum-scarum scheme, one proposed moreover by a total stranger half her age, I was even more amazed at my own good luck.

"You have only three days to learn the system," I said. "I should tell you it is not gambling—what we will have to do is sit there hour after hour, day after day. It is very hard work. You'll have to have some pretty intensive coaching."

"Come as early as you like tomorrow. By the way, are you interested in insects?"

"I beg your pardon?"

"It's my hobby, collecting moths and beetles and that sort of thing. I've got *cases* of them. Will there be time in France for me to look for specimens?"

"You'll be free in the mornings," I said, tactfully declining an invitation to examine her scarab beetles.

Only five days later, in August, 1957, this unusual woman and I stepped out of the brilliant Riviera sunshine and climbed the gloomy stairs to the swing doors of the Casino Municipale. By that time I had realized that Mrs. Harper-Biggs was one of those middle-aged, middle-class women who find that comparative affluence is no compensation for boredom, a tweedy English lady faced with that most poignant question: Is *this* the best life has to offer? I daresay that if I had suggested going up the Orinoco by canoe, she would have agreed just as readily. Escape was all that mattered.

We took our seats at one of the tables. The French were still using old francs and at one table the minimum stake was only 200 francs—about 4 shillings in those days (60 cents), 20 new pence today.

The low stakes puzzled Mrs. Harper-Biggs. While we waited for the table staff to take up their positions she said: "I always thought these places were for the rich."

"Not at all. They don't care about the social tone of the clientele—even if you're not wearing a tie, they'll lend you one. You have to be a known criminal, a prostitute or on their blacklist to be refused admittance."

"Yet it looks rather imposing."

"Believe me, the decor isn't designed to attract the blue blood of Europe. The flunkeys, the chandeliers, the marble pillars—they're all part of a psychological gambit. If the atmosphere were that of a Wild West saloon, with drunkenness and revelry on all sides, you might begin to suspect that the gambling could be less than honest. But

what possible harm could befall you in the pomp and circumstance of all this?"

"Are these people just devious or do they cheat as well?"

"They don't have to. All the odds are in their favour. Every mathematical and psychological advantage acquired over a hundred years is being turned against you at this very moment."

We placed our first stakes of the day, both of us putting down 200-franc chips to start nine solid hours of gambling. Her very lack of emotion helped Mrs. Harper-Biggs ignore the many distractions of the casino. In three days she had acquired a good grasp of the theory of the Fitzroy and had no difficulty with her three staking columns and her combinations of colour sequences. As always the Fitzroy provided small but seductively consistent wins. Towards the end of the day the croupiers began to take an interest in us, but after a while they shrugged and shifted their attention elsewhere. It takes a great deal to excite an experienced casino croupier. He has seen all the world can offer in the way of human ingenuity, greed and stupidity.

When Mrs. Harper-Biggs and I left the table at midnight and cashed in our chips, we had won about £200 ($560). On an empty table we divided our bundle of franc notes and then walked across the square to the nearest café—the Massena—for a drink. She had a gin and tonic while I had a grenadine. We were an unlikely couple to be sitting tête-a-tête in the warm air of a Mediterranean night, myself aged twenty-seven, dressed as always in a dark suit, white shirt and bow tie, she in her middle forties, an inch taller than myself, dressed in a tweed suit that was not so much old-fashioned as timeless and a hat of Edwardian vintage.

"I must admit, Mr. Leigh, I really am amazed," she said, for all her amazement sounding just as unmoved as

before. "You said we would win about a hundred pounds each and that's exactly what's happened. I didn't believe you could predict our profits so accurately."

"Ah yes, but then I've gone into this subject rather deeply, you see," I said expansively. "Other people look at the roulette table and what do they see? A green baize layout with thirty-six numbered squares—like a bingo card."

"I suppose it is when you think of it."

"Yes, but a very deadly game. What I see is a machine for taking the money of mugs. Those people round the table looking so worldly and sophisticated—most of them are nutcases, Mrs. Harper-Biggs, absolute idiots!"

"Doesn't that include us?"

"We're not stupid enough to be betting on single numbers at thirty-five to one, are we? With our staking patterns and our colour combinations we're trying to make the percentages favour us. Percentages, Mrs. Harper-Biggs, that's what it's all about."

Even that phlegmatic lady was impressed.

"But how did *you* come to these theories, Mr. Leigh? I mean, why don't all the other players follow your example?"

I raised a nonchalant hand. "I'm obsessed with *winning*, not living out a gambler's fantasies. Everybody will tell you it's impossible to win consistently at roulette: but the bank's only advantage on even chances is one point four percent—in theory. How could a tiny percentage like that account for the vast numbers who've been ruined at the roulette table? The simple answer is that they gambled while the bank played percentages— not just the pure mathematics of the wheel but all the other advantages in the bank's favour: sober croupiers against tipsy players, unlimited bank capital against the individual's limited reserves and—most crucial of all—the inhuman patience of the bank against the emotional

fallibility of the player. That's the whole point of our system—to remove intuition and hunches and all that nonsense from our minds. We do our thinking in advance and when we're at the table we are as logical and cold-blooded as the bank."

Unfortunately there was a lot more to it than that, as I would later discover.

For several days the method worked exactly according to theory. Starting each day with a capital of £100 each, we played from 3 P.M. until midnight and would then come away from the cash desk with a profit of around £100 each. I began to believe it could go on forever. Each day became a carbon copy of the day before. Mrs. Harper-Biggs spent her mornings on the hills behind the town looking for unusual insects, which she collected. She had scores of them in little bottles in her room and was always arriving at lunchtime with exciting tales of the hunt. I passed my mornings meandering about the town, having an occasional aperitif in the cafés, enjoying myself in the study of the teeming human life. We would meet at the Café Massena each day and take in the passing scene over lunch, a strangely matched English couple sitting among the dice players and the sun worshippers. Apart from roulette we did not have much in common, and as she was liable to fill any gap in the conversation with dissertations on insect life I generally tried to confine it to casinos. She wasn't particularly interested in roulette theory, but she did like to hear about fraud and crime. Shocking her deep-seated sense of propriety became a sort of game with me.

"Oh, there have been weird and wonderful attempts to cheat the casinos," I would say. "One was rather clever. In the old days suicide was fairly common and the casinos became very sensitive to bad publicity. With all this cash floating about they have always been a magnet for con-

men. The fake-suicide dodge needed two sharpies working in a team with a fair amount of capital, a starting pistol
and a bottle of tomato sauce. They would both stake a
thousand pounds, one on red, one on black, so that between them they never actually lost any money. The one
who lost would break down in tears and rush out into the
gardens, fire the starting pistol, pour ketchup over himself
and play dead. The other one would tell the table staff he'd
overheard him saying he was ruined. An ambulance would
be called, but meanwhile the casino officials would rush
out into the gardens and stuff sums of money into the
dead man's pockets so that nobody could blame the casino
for having destroyed him."

"Are you sure you're not—"

"Mrs. Harper-Biggs, there is no limit to human devious-
ness when one is this close to a veritable ocean of money."

"I suppose they were foreigners," she said firmly.

On our seventh day the Chef de Casino, the same
swarthy, balding man who had laughed at my father, let
me know our activities had been noted.

"Monsieur," he said jokingly, "your profits each day
have been so consistent I think we should come to a
simple arrangement whereby you merely report to the
cash desk at midnight and collect the same amount without the inconvenience of playing."

"Ah yes, wonderful idea," I replied. We both laughed,
though I was not particularly pleased that he had noticed
us.

The very next day Mrs. Harper-Biggs began to crack.
"I can't stand all those Italians," she announced abruptly
at lunch in the café.

"I don't understand," I said, glancing round at the
other tables.

"All those Italians who've started coming to the
casino."

"They're only day parties from the border towns. Why do they bother you?"

"They're noisy. They stink of garlic. I find them most distasteful."

It was not, of course, the Italians who were bothering her, but the strain of method roulette over such long hours days after day, which requires a degree of will-power and stamina far beyond that needed for most occupations. However, we played as usual that day and won around £100 each ($280).

The following day at lunch she issued a strange ultimatum.

"I'm not prepared to go on playing with these Italians," she said. "There is an excellent casino at Leopoldville in the Belgian Congo. I want to go there."

The whisky shook in my glass.

"The Belgian Congo?"

"Herbert and I lived there for some years. The casino is first-class, and there are no Italians, thank God."

The years have taught me patience with people who do not share my obsession or my stamina, perhaps taught me they are fortunate to be better balanced psychologically than myself, but I was an impatient young man then. What right did she have to break up a trip which was vindicating my theories so profitably?

"I like this casino," I said coldly. "I have no intention of changing the venue, particularly for some sweaty equatorial hothouse."

We argued for an hour and reached a compromise. From the next day we would switch to another casino in Nice, a privately run establishment much more opulent than the Municipale. In other words, no noisy day trippers from Italy.

Though the 100-franc admission charge was the same, this other place had higher social pretensions than the

Municipale—certainly the drink prices were much grander. The staff was dressed in eighteenth-century attire, knee breeches, stockings, powdered wigs—just another psychological gimmick to lure players into a false sense of security. At 3 P.M. the following day we took our seats and began staking.

The wheel was spinning for only the second time when a large group of Italians made a conspicuous entrance. Mrs. Harper-Biggs went paler than usual. Even then she might have survived, but within a few more spins she hit a "run" on the four colour combinations she was handling. In the Fitzroy system, a run is an adverse sequence which causes the figures in the staking and imaginary "loss" columns to assume large proportions as the player endeavours to recoup his losses. Mrs. Harper-Biggs' stakes quickly went up to £30 and £40.

Then she faltered. With a complicated system, any break in concentration is enough to cause a mental blockage. The paper calculations become terrifyingly difficult, and panic paralyzes the brain.

"I'm feeling faint," she said, getting up from the table. I hurried after her. "Let's have a drink," I said, leading her to the bar. She said it was the heat making her feel giddy, then claimed it was the smell of garlic from those confounded Italians. Finally she looked at me and said aggressively: "What you really need is not a partner but a human zombie."

She went back to Bournemouth the next day. I went to Cannes with the £300 ($840) I had left of our winnings. I wanted to find another partner, for there was no way that I could handle the eight permutations of colour sequences on my own. The local paper refused to accept any advertisement. I returned to Bournemouth not so much dispirited as damnably annoyed at having been let down by the human element.

• 3

Over the next two years my obsession became overwhelming. I spent patient hours training people to play the Fitzroy system and made several sallies to the south of France. Each time disaster struck in one form or another and I had to return. On one occasion after a promising start when we won £300 we encountered a terrible adverse sequence and lost both our winnings and our capital.

More often than not, however, it was the personalities of the individual members which prevented success. The ability to play, in Mrs. Harper-Biggs' phrase, like "a human zombie" over long hours in the south of France, when the attendant glamours of wine, women and song are constantly beckoning, is rare.

The closest I came to success was with a team of eight in Nice. On our first day's play we won over £1,300 ($3,600). As I sat having breakfast on the balcony of my hotel room the next morning, contemplating the orange groves bathed in sunlight and the fortune we were about to make, a member of the team came to my room and told me that he was, in fact, a police officer who had been ordered to investigate me and my team to make sure there was no fraud involved.

I was appalled. "And you have been disabused of that idea?" I asked curtly.

"Yes, I have. I realize it's all quite genuine now. I'm returning to Bournemouth. I'm sorry for any embarrassment you may have been caused."

"Have you informed the other members of the team?"

"Yes. I had to explain why I was leaving. But I did tell them you were cleared of all suspicion."

"But they didn't know I was under suspicion," I said angrily. "You know as well as I do that when a man is dragged through the courts and then told he is innocent his reputation is never really restored. Is it?"

"I can't comment on that."

"No, I didn't expect you could. Well, perhaps you will allow me to comment that you don't emerge very creditably, Inspector. Now, perhaps the less we say to each other, the better. Good-bye."

When I joined the team for lunch that day the atmosphere was notably tense. A conversation ensued in which four members of the team said they couldn't afford any hint of scandal and were returning forthwith.

With less than half the team remaining we had little choice but to pack our bags and do likewise.

Back in England while total depression set in, something happened which, though I did not know it at the time, was to change my life. One afternoon while browsing through a secondhand bookshop, my eye was caught by a small volume with faded brown bindings and an intriguing title, *How To Really Beat the Bank at Monte Carlo*. It had been published in 1926, the author Lord Beresford; obviously one of those self-indulgent memoirs published at the writer's expense. I bought it for sixpence and put it in my overcoat pocket. That night at a party I found myself talking to someone about roulette (I talked to *everybody* about roulette) and happened to show him Lord Beresford's book.

"I'd like to read that," he said. "If I promise to let you have it back in a week, will you lend it to me?"

I let him borrow the book and forgot about it for the time being. A fortnight or so later I ran into him again and asked him when I would get it back.

He looked at me oddly and said, "But surely you remember—I gave it back to you the last time we met, in the bar of the Norfolk Hotel. You must remember."

"I don't, actually."

"Sure you're not hitting the bottle a bit hard, old boy?" were his parting words.

This entirely accurate remark sowed the seeds of a radical alteration in my thinking which was eventually to reach a successful climax when I led the twelve to victory in Nice. I was sure my system could work, yet all my efforts had been ruined by the type of people I was forced to use as partners. Sober, reliable citizens were not interested in gaming forays to France, and even if I could find them there was no way I could train them properly in real conditions before putting them to the test. It was also obvious that system roulette could not be run by committee. Yet how could I assume dictatorial powers over people when they had all the capital? At the time I felt I was finished with roulette—finished every way as well. I resolved to cut my losses and move to London to try to knuckle down to some kind of career and cure myself of this insane obsession with making gambling history. I was unaware that The Sign had already manifested itself.

Lord Beresford's little memoir, bought for sixpence from a secondhand dealer, was The Sign. It turned up almost four years later, in circumstances that leave me in no doubt that Fate had chosen roulette as my destiny. Consider the evidence before you judge me a crank.

I had spent those four years in London trying to settle

· 53 ·

down in business careers of various kinds, some success-ful, like a dabble in the property market, some disastrous, like a car-hire scheme I floated. But even when I was doing well my heart was not in commerce. Those early roulette fiascos had toughened me considerably, however, and I was no longer given to introspective suffering, my philosophy being that as we are here for only a short time, we might as well have as smooth a passage as possible. I had dismissed my addiction to roulette as a fantasy of youth. Even when gaming was made legal in Britain and a casino seemed to sprout round every corner I was never once tempted to enter one. For me there was no pleasure in the rigmarole of betting, only in the challenge of out-witting the men who control the machine.

Then I fell in love. Her name was Pauline—petite, dark-haired, only twenty years old. I was thirty-six. We met at a party in South Kensington in May, 1965.

Her first words to me were: "I've been watching you all evening—you drink far too much whisky."

We talked for an hour. She telephoned me next morn-ing, and we saw each other several times in the next few days. A couple of weeks later we were strolling by the picturesque church in The Boltons off Old Brompton Road. I hadn't planned such a drastic step, but on the spur of the moment, the sun shining, a warm breeze on our faces, I asked her to marry me. I can only ascribe her acceptance to the romantic stimuli of the day's climate, for I was no great catch. Whatever my last business ven-ture had been it was a flop. I had no job, no prospects, and was barely able to pay my part of the rent of a flat I was sharing with three other people. Not that any of this wor-ried me in the slightest.

We borrowed a friend's car and drove to Ryde on the Isle of Wight to meet Pauline's parents.

Inevitably the moment came when her father, one of the stiff old school, enquired about my prospects.

"I have none at all," I said, preparing for the storm.

"Well, tell me about yourself."

"I can tell you about a wide variety of disasters if they are of any interest," I said. I did. I may even have given him a few philosophical musings on work being spiritual death and the sheepishness of most people in allowing themselves to be submerged in jobs in which they found no chance to use their energies or imaginations.

To my surprise he burst out laughing. Then he told me about *his* more startling escapades. Far from the stuffy man he appeared, he had been one of those balk-at-nothing adventurers who were responsible for this country's former greatness. He had worked in the nitrate fields of Chile, fought a duel in Valparaiso, hunted tigers in Sumatra, pursued adventure round the world.

Pauline and I were married at Binstead Church, Isle of Wight, in a torrential downpour. We drove back to our flat in London. No sooner had we crossed the threshold than Pauline said sweetly, "What are we going to do now?"

It was a devastating moment. The little money I had was rapidly dwindling, and I had given no thought to how to make more. The euphoria of irresponsibility cleared like a fog before a gale as I looked down into her trusting face, which radiated absolute confidence in her new husband's ability to give her the best of all possible worlds.

My new scheme was to rent a large Georgian house and, unbeknown to the property company from which we leased it, sublet it before signing any contract.

Within two days of placing an advertisement we had three paying guests, a professional lady from Australia and two male bank executives. In another week we had rented five of the bedrooms. I was paying £30 a week in rent and collecting roughly £85, which gave us a substantial

roof over our heads and £50 a week to live on. It was enough. And it was quite legal.

Then, one afternoon while she was sorting out the contents of an old chest of drawers we had had to store at her parents' home while house hunting, Pauline found The Sign: Lord Beresford's book on how to beat the bank at Monte Carlo.

"How the hell did it get in there?" I asked myself. I hadn't seen the book for at least four years. I must have had it wrapped in a bundle of papers in that drawer ever since it had been returned to me by my friend in the bar of the Norfolk Hotel, the night I was so drunk I hadn't remembered meeting him.

Never having opened the book since the day I'd bought it in Boscombe Arcade, I sat down to read it there and then. I was still reading at three the next morning. Lord Beresford, whoever he might have been, was no hare-brained crackpot. He gave a cool and factual assessment of roulette and his explanation for the failure of all players to win at it consistently. By the time I had finished his monograph for the second or third time that night the old fever was raging in me. At last I saw how the wheel could be beaten!

Like myself, Lord Beresford had been puzzled by the universal failure of all roulette systems; he reasoned that there had to be another reason, apart from zero's percentage, for the table's apparent inability to lose. This tiny mathematical advantage could hardly be responsible for the vast number of people ruined by roulette. So he proceeded to analyze the "career" of a typical method player using the popular system known as *montant et demontant*.

Let us say he stakes £1 on red. If he wins he has £2. He takes back £1 and stakes the pound he has just won

on red again. If he loses the pound he then stakes £2. If he loses £2, he stakes £3, always increasing his stake by one unit. When he next wins he decreases his stake by one unit, so that if he has £3 on the table and he wins his next bet will be £2. It's a simple progression. He increases his stake by one unit after a loss and decreases it by one unit after a win.

Beresford imagined a method player starting with a capital of £1,000 and betting in units of £1. He plays for five hours each day, which on a French table gives him 150 spins to work on. Betting on any of the six even chances (red, black; odd, even; high, low), he will almost certainly win an average of £75 a day—in theory, the method being geared to win half a unit per spin.

On his first day the Beresford player makes his theoretical profit for the first three hours when he hits an adverse run, in which black predominates. Having to increase his stake by £1 after each loss, he is soon betting in high stakes. Before he recovers his previous losses he has to stake £300 of his capital. Nevertheless, after a further two hours' play he is able to finish with his £75 profit. However—and this is the crucial point—in the five hours he was at the table he needed to risk £300 of his own money, which meant that the bank had at that stage four times as much of his money as he now has of the bank's money when he leaves.

The second day, the Beresford player is immediately hit with an adverse sequence of black predominating. He has to stake £450 of his money to recover his initial losses. However, at the end of the session he has made his £75 profit.

On the third day his profits go according to plan for four and a half hours, then he runs into an adverse sequence of such magnitude (black predominating by 3 to

1) that he has to stake all of his £1,000 capital in an attempt to recover his losses. He fails. He loses the £1,000 plus his accumulated profits of £225.

Through all this the bank has merely been playing a waiting game, quite content to let him take £225 of its capital because it knows that sooner or later an adverse sequence will deprive him of his profits and his entire capital as well. Why wouldn't the player give up before that happens? Because he is a gambler, and the bank knows his psychology. It is always willing to speculate £225 to win £1,000, for there are very few *gamblers* temperamentally capable of applying common sense, especially if they are hooked on the quasilogic of a system. All systems fail, no matter how ingeniously designed, because the adverse sequences cause the player to risk sums out of all proportion to his modest wins.

All known systems, that is. Yet here in his book, with one of those devastatingly simple insights that always make one wonder why nobody thought of it before, Beresford put forward an idea that literally turned the tables on the bank. All known systems were devised to minimize losses in the first instance and then to produce small but consistent wins. As long as the wheel produced a pattern of results roughly in accordance with the laws of chance all went well. But the wheel has never heard of the laws of chance. Where that little ivory ball falls is purely arbitrary. Over infinity the incidence of red and black will be equal but over a whole day the laws of probability make it certain that one will predominate over longer or shorter periods. That is where the caution built into all systems becomes of no avail.

All right, said Lord Beresford, why not play the system in *reverse order?* Suppose the player with £1,000 should *decrease* his stakes after a loss and increase them after a *win*. At one stroke everything has been changed.

Instead of setting out to win £75 a day the player sets out prepared to lose £75 a day. He makes no attempt to chase his losses—the basic philosophy behind most systems. If he bets £1 on red and it loses, he then places a smaller bet. If that loses, he reduces his stake once again, the amount being determined by whichever staking system it is he chooses to reverse.

In effect he is now playing the bank's role. And the bank, compelled to play the system against the player, becomes subject to all the disadvantages inherent in systems. Furthermore, whereas the player can lose only his capital of £1,000, the table is at risk for virtually all it carries, which is normally £5,000. The table cannot get up and walk away when it chooses.

The obvious snag, said Beresford, was having to resign yourself to a dreary succession of small losses over a period of a week or more before a favourable sequence occurred. However, when that sequence does appear only two things can happen. Either the table is broken, that is to say fresh reserves of capital have to be brought up, which means it would have lost some £5,000. Or alternatively—and this seemed more likely—the upper staking limit will be reached and the player prohibited from taking his staking progression any further. His probable winnings in this eventuality would be around £2,000.

I read this explanation again and again and failed to see any major flaw in Beresford's reasoning. He had taken an apparently immutable law, that systems must fail, and found the way to turn it to the player's advantage. All he was asking the player to do was come to the table with a different psychological approach to gambling, not to look for consistent wins but to adopt the inhuman patience of the bank.

By this time I was literally aching with a premonition —no, a *certainty*—that this tattered old sixpenny book was

the answer. Not that I was so enthused that I could see myself going all the way with Lord Beresford, who must be given due credit for a truly aristocratic disdain for such petty ambitions as the mere winning of a few thousand pounds. In his last chapter he revealed, quite simply, that he had thought up this scheme with a view to becoming the *owner* of the casino at Monte Carlo. The way to do this, he claimed, was to find the most dangerous roulette system, dangerous from the player's point of view—any system that could be shown to have caused an outstanding number of financial disasters and suicides—to apply it in reverse, to select and train no fewer than three hundred players, pack the tables at Monte Carlo and compel the casino to play the wrong end of a dangerous system against three hundred opponents simultaneously.

This trained army would win so much that casino shares would drop to rock bottom on the Paris Bourse. Then Beresford and friends would buy up the shares and make themselves effective owners of the most famous casino in the world. He thought all this could be achieved in twenty-eight days!

I have never met anyone who could tell me anything about Lord Beresford. He sounded more like a financier than a true gambler though perhaps not a financier to whom one might have entrusted one's life savings with any great confidence. Yet the roulette part of his theory made sense. It struck at the very flaw which had ruined all my previous attempts to beat the wheel.

All I had to do now was discover the most dangerous system ever devised.

For the next two or three days I took myself to the secondhand bookshops of Charing Cross Road in the West End. Most of the literature available concentrated on the social life of Monte Carlo between 1900 and 1925, the

scandals, the financial disasters, the suicides. Only obliquely did any of the books I browsed through deal with the actual mechanics of roulette, but after a great deal of reading the name of one particular system came to the fore.

That name was Labouchère.

Named not after a Frenchman as the name might suggest but after one of Queen Victoria's ministers, the Labouchère was second to none in the suicide stakes. Like most methods it is based on the even chances, that is, the six bets (red or black, odd or even, high or low), which pay even money winnings of £1 for every £1 staked. It has an insidious ability to lull the player into a sense of euphoria by the constant winning of small sums. Simplicity makes it even more ruinously attractive. Pauline, a complete roulette novice, picked it up without much difficulty. I sat her in the lounge with a notepad and pencil and told her to write a line of figures, 1, 2, 3, 4, down the left-hand side of the page, which then looked this way:

1
2
3
4

"In this system you always stake the sum of the figures at either end of the line—so what would your first stake be?" I asked her.

"Um—one and four—five?"

"Correct. You're staking five units on the first spin."

"What am I staking them on?"

"Any of the six even chances, it doesn't matter which. Let's say black. You've staked five units, let's call them pounds. You win. When you win you automatically delete

the figures at either end of the line. What does that leave you with?"

Her notepad then looked like this:

~~1~~
2
3
~~4~~

"So your next stake is—"

She thought for a moment. "There are only two figures so they must be the end figures. Two and three—I'm staking five again, am I?"

"Very good. Let's say black comes up again and you win. What do you do now?"

"I'm supposed to delete the figures at the end of the line but—"

"That's right, delete them."

What she had now was this:

~~1~~
~~2~~
~~3~~
~~4~~

"I've nothing left," she said.

"So that line is finished with. You've had a short winning sequence and you've won two bets of five pounds at even money—that gives you ten pounds. Now you start all over again."

1
2
3
4

"This time you stake five pounds as before but red comes up and you lose. In that case you always add the amount of your last stake to the end of the line, which is now

1
2
3
4
5

So what do you stake?"

"One plus five—six?"

"That's it. When you win you cross off the figures at either end of the line. When you lose you add the stake to the end of the line. If you went on losing you can see how the line would lengthen and your stakes would increase, always betting a little more to get your losses back when a win comes along. Every time the line is crossed out completely you have won ten units. You have only to follow the two basic rules and the figures will tell you what to stake next.

"You see, the limit to the calculations most people can do in their heads is doubling up—"

"Surely that would be a lot simpler?"

I told her the old gambler's story about the grains of corn. An ancient philosopher had done his king a great service and was offered any reward he named. He told the king he would like as many grains of corn as it took to double up on each square of the chessboard, one grain on the first square, two on the second, four on the third and so on up to the sixty-fourth square. The king saw this as a fairly modest request—until he started putting corn on the board. Then he discovered that to double up all the way round sixty-four squares would require

something like ten trillion grains of corn, more than there was in all the barns in the kingdom.

"That's what happens when you double up," I said. "Ruination."

Hiram Maxim, of machine-gun fame, said there was no way to win at roulette unless you actually stole from the table. You would need *unlimited* capital to go on doubling until the law of averages let you win. And there is also the crucial factor of the table limit. If you could eventually recoup your losses with one large bet doubling up might be possible—but most tables have a maximum stake, say £200 on the even chances. You would need a phenomenally long winning run at bets of £200 to get back all you had lost while your stakes were going up to the limit. Even Einstein could not see a way of winning at roulette.

"Well? Is this system any better?" Pauline asked.

"Not at all. It's damnably destructive. I've seen people working up their stakes to thousands of units—and to get that far they must have been losing on the grand scale. Yet they were still trying to win a miserable ten units!"

With the perplexity of the innocent she asked, "But why are people so insane as to use a system like that if they know it's going to ruin them?"

"Small wins on a steady basis. You're deceived into thinking the system is infallible and as a result you are trapped. When you hit a losing run you chase your losses far beyond what you can afford because you're convinced you cannot lose. Hence all the suicides."

"I suppose people get carried away in all the excitement. I still don't see how your idea makes any difference —'reversing,' you called it, didn't you?"

"Well, playing the system the orthodox way means playing for small but steady wins and taking big risks when a losing sequence comes up. Suppose you went to the table prepared for small steady *losses* and then seized

on a favorable sequence to maximize your wins. All you
have to do is change those two rules. Try it again—write
the same line on your pad." She wrote the figures on a
clean page.

1
2
3
4

"You stake five on black and it wins. This time you
add the amount of the winning stake to the line, which
becomes . . ."

1
2
3
4
5

"Now—your stake will be what?"
"One plus five—six?"
"Correct. On the next spin you win again."
"I add the amount of the winning stake again?"
"Yes." The line became

1
2
3
4
5
6

"Now your stake will be—"
"One plus six—seven."
"Right. But this time you lose."
"And I score out the end figures?"

"Yes." The line now read

1̸
2
3
4
5
6̸

"All right. Your next stake is two plus five—seven. Only you lose again."
The line became

1̸
2̸
3
4̸
5̸
6̸

If she won with her next spin, the line would change to

1̸
2̸
'3
4
5̸
6̸
7

Once a figure has been crossed off it is forgotten; 3, 4, 7 was the effective line. I told her that she had lost again. She scored off 3 and 7.

"But I've only got one figure left," she said.

"That's right. Four. So that's your next stake. If you lose again you cross off the four and you have deleted the

whole line. If you win, you write down another 4 and you stake 8. No matter how long it has become, once it's crossed off entirely you have lost only ten units. This would be the rule, hour after hour, starting new lines, winning a little, losing a little, finally crossing off the whole line and then starting again,

1
2
3
4

but having lost only ten units. What the orthodox method player doesn't realize is that the very caution of the normal system *is* its weakness. He can *never* win enough to compensate for what he loses in a major adverse sequence, because he is crossing his line out when he has *won* ten units. His bets only go up when he is losing. What we would do is turn the orthodox system upside-down, still having the figures to control the staking pattern but going for maximum winnings rather than minimum losses."

"I think I see now—but who do you mean by *we?*"

"One small ad in the papers and we'll have no shortage of volunteers, believe you me. Trouble is, half of them will be drunks or rascals."

At dinner that night I was preoccupied with that same old problem—how to find reliable people. What I needed was a team exactly like Pauline—respectable, staid, sober, loyal—and preferably people who had never seen a roulette table. How on earth to find them, though? My Bournemouth advertisement had only hinted at gambling, yet it always attracted eccentrics. This time I would have to advertise in the national papers, where I had no convenient cousins. I wanted people to play roulette, but no newspaper would allow me to mention roulette. I wanted people who could leave England for an indefinite period but I didn't want idle playboys. I wanted people with

some capital, but the newspapers would assume that any advertisement asking for money involved a confidence trick.

Then I had an idea. I would let the applicants eliminate themselves!

Of course! I could make a *virtue* out of the fact that I couldn't advertise directly. I would put them through such an obstacle course that all the fly-by-nights and chancers would drop out along the way. And I would save myself the drudgery of tramping the streets with a toy wheel in a carrier bag, being shown the door as soon as I mentioned gambling.

The wording of that ad was positively artistic.

FRENCH RIVIERA. A LIMITED NUMBER OF VACANCIES OF A CLERICAL NATURE OCCUR IN A GROUP TO BE FORMED ON THE CÔTE D'AZUR. SOME SPEED AT FIGUREWORK ESSENTIAL. APPLICANTS WILL BE EXPECTED TO SUPPLY IMPECCABLE REFERENCES. BOX . . .

Artistic? It was accepted without hesitation by the advertising departments of the *Daily Telegraph, The Times, The Sunday Times,* the *Sunday Telegraph* and the *Guardian!*

As I was phoning the newspaper offices the next morning Pauline looked more and more worried. A brain wave was one thing, but to put it into reality seemed to her extremely risky.

"Do you really think you'll get any answers?" she asked.

"By the score," I said confidently.

If I had known of the deluge to come it's possible that even I might have felt a certain chill about the lower extremities. Experience had taught me there is no easy money to be made at roulette, but to call what happened when my advertisements appeared a nightmare would be to give bad dreams a good name.

4

While waiting for the first replies I bought a proper six-teen-inch roulette wheel for 25 guineas ($75). With the wheel came a cloth layout and chips, as real a setup as one could approximate without investing around £10,000 ($28,000) in genuine casino equipment

For the next two days I ran a series of experiments to see how long it would take a single player working the Reverse Labouchère, as I decided to call my variant, either to break the table or reach the maximum staking limit. Assuming that a player worked twelve hours a day— that is, 360 spins of the wheel—I crammed a week's work into a morning, positively devouring notepads as I recorded sequence after sequence. The obsession became all-devouring. I could see that Pauline was going round the bend but I could only trust in her sense of loyalty to give her patience—at that stage I was grimly prepared to sacrifice *everything* to make this scheme work.

On average I found that the player would go on losing for five solid days, playing twelve hours a day, before he had a favorable sequence on the sixth day. There are six even-chance bets on the table: red (*rouge*) and black (*noir*); even numbers (*pair*) and odd numbers (*impair*); high (*passe*—the numbers from nineteen to thirty-six) and low (*manque*—the numbers from one to eighteen). Six people

covering these simultaneously would give the group every likelihood of one winning progression per day's gaming. Four-hour shifts would be ideal—which meant that I needed three teams of six, eighteen players in all.

"Won't they be put off by the idea of having to supply character references?" Pauline asked doubtfully.

"I hope so—the ones who aren't willing to work at it, anyway. After all, darling, Everest wasn't climbed by civil servants with a fetish for tea breaks, was it?"

The advertisements appeared, and for the first few days the letters could be counted in dozens. By the end of the week they were coming by the sackload. The whole house seemed to be swamped. This could have been more daunting than a meager response, the sheer weight of replies giving the operation an almost frightening dimension. However, I could only swallow hard and press on. I decided to hire two full-time typists from a local agency. I bought two desks for them to work at, two Olivetti typewriters and three filing cabinets. What's a little expense and inconvenience when you're planning to make gambling history?

Once the two girls had started replying to all the applicants, arranging a schedule of initial meetings at our house, my next job was to decide which of London's casinos would best serve as a training ground. It had to be reasonably easy to reach, large enough to accommodate the group and to sustain heavy losses without complaint, and it also had to be reputable, which was not always the case in those wide-open years when gaming was first legalized in Britain in January, 1961.

I bought a copy of *What's On,* a weekly guide to London night life, and ticked off the casinos that sounded most likely. I visited a dozen in all. Having been used to the high standards common to French casinos, this process was an eye-opener. Some of the casinos were too flashy

and opulent, to the trained eye an obvious indication that they were out to fleece their patrons. Some were tatty and full of drunks, the Gaming Board not then in existence to ban alcohol, and some ruled themselves out by the predominance of scantily clad girls on the floor, naked flesh there not to delight the eye but to distract the players.

After visiting a dozen, I eventually picked on a gaming club I shall call the Regency. It seemed a sober enough establishment, impressively functional, most of the clientele being nouveau riche but with enough of what I would call the real McCoy type of gambler to indicate that the tables were honestly run.

Now I had the interviewing to do: twelve hundred people had replied to our box numbers, and my typists had replied to them all. With so many people interested, I could afford to be choosy, so I had made it far from easy to join the group. The applicants would have to undergo three separate interviews, which would mean three separate trips to my home in Twickenham, and would have to supply three character references, all of which my girls would write to. Then I would insist on a month's coaching and practice at my house before they could set foot in a casino. The interviews would weed out the lazy ones, the character references would eliminate the shady customers and the month's training would put off the easy-money brigade.

Over the next seven weeks I actually interviewed 951 men and women, a monumental task that all the money in all the casinos in the world would hardly induce me to repeat. The common misconception that professional gambling is an idler's escape from hard work always amuses me in a wry sort of way. Any person tempted to mastermind a gaming coup must be prepared for labours which, if suggested to the average trade unionist, would cause a general strike. My first appointment of each day was at

10 A.M., and with only half an hour for lunch I went on seeing people until nine at night. I usually went to bed in a state of collapse.

The necessarily oblique wording of my advertisements brought me many applicants who thought they were being offered a nice clerical job in the sun. Most of them took the news that I was recruiting for a gaming syndicate with the politeness one would like to think is still an English characteristic, though a few were a trifle irate.

"This is a bloody cheek, dragging me all the way to Twickenham for a fly-by-night gaming caper," raved one particularly disappointed lotus-eater.

To those who neither ranted nor turned tail I made the same formal speech. (Complete formality, I had decided, was to be the keynote.)

"I am looking for people to form a team which will attempt systematically and continuously to win money from casinos. You probably think that all roulette systems fail. My basic premise is that I have found a way of making the bank play the system and the player reap all the advantages the bank normally has. It will require from you a little capital and a lot of hard work, a month's training here and then practical experience of real conditions in a London casino—possibly three months of preparation in all before we are ready to travel to the south of France, probably late this year."

Quite a number began to nod their heads enthusiastically at this stage, but I had learned my lesson the hard way.

"Don't make up your mind now," I would continue. "Here is my card. Go away and think it over and then ring me if you are still interested, and we can arrange a second interview. You will also be asked to supply the names and addresses of three people to whom I can write for a character reference."

This was pure flannel, of course—on a venture like this they should have been asking *me* for written evidence of my good character. I presumed that unmitigated drunkards and scoundrels would be put off by the thought of having to produce independent testimony to their social worthiness. Those early abortive trips had taught me that nobody can tell from one formal interview if a man or woman is reliable and honest. (Once we had started narrowing down the numbers, my girls did write off for these references, though this was done largely to maintain the note of respectable formality.)

What sort of people turned up? Every kind. Young, old, successful, shabby, loud, meek—apart from any *obvious* ministers of religion, almost every other trade and profession was represented in that avalanche.

One rather timid, grey-haired lady in her early fifties listened deferentially to my formal declaration of intent and then said: "Oh. I thought the advertisement was for a job in the south of France."

"I'm sorry, madam," I replied. "I could not be specific in the ad but you will agree that it does not offer paid employment."

"I don't understand—how can you take people to the Côte d'Azur if it isn't to work for a business?"

"We would hope to win money, Mrs.—er—Heppenstall. As I've explained, I think I know how to make a profit playing roulette. I'm not guaranteeing anything, only that there is a strong likelihood that one would come out of the experience with more money than when one went in."

"Oh. It isn't what I expected. You see, my husband died in February—it's so difficult at my age. I was a secretary, but that was twenty-four years ago. Most employers think I'm out of date."

"I'm sorry. Have you come far?"

"From Hastings actually." Her face was so mournful I had a momentary impulse to refund her train fare. Only momentary. There were many sadder cases than hers if I had been tempted to do welfare work.

"I'm sorry you were inconvenienced," I said, taking her to the front door.

"Oh no, it was very good of you to see me." She walked off down the drive, a small woman in a dark green coat, walking slowly with short steps.

Careful as I was not to make snap judgments about individuals in that human Niagara flowing through our house, one man did make an impression on me from the start. His name was Blake. He looked like a grown-up Billy Bunter, the schoolboy glutton of English comic-books, but was immaculately dressed in a pinstripe suit with a waistcoat, his black hair brushed flat. His manners were almost eccentrically formal for someone his age.

Having heard my preamble, he fixed me with a cold, patrician eye and said, in clipped tones: "Mr. Leigh, you are wasting my time. I thought this was a serious proposition."

Something about him, a genuine steeliness behind the podgy features and stiff manners, made me instinctively feel that he merited special attention.

"Just hear me out," I said. "This method compels the bank to play the system against the player. If you know anything about roulette you will be aware that nobody has ever tried to implement a system in reverse before."

"I know little about roulette except that all systems fail," he said disdainfuly. "Good day to you."

"You've come ten miles—why not hear a bit more about it?" I said. He nodded curtly, still poised to rise. "I've spent the better part of my adult life trying to find a winning method for roulette," I went on. "I've taken all sorts of people to this casino in Nice. Sometimes we won,

and then my associates cracked under the strain. Sometimes I discovered too late that they were dipsomaniacs or womanizers or straightforward lunatics. This time I'm going for reliability. I'm not promising easy money—far from it. But it would be a chance to do something unique in gaming history—to be the very first. The idea of reversing the system is—"

"All systems fail!"

"Agreed. But all known systems are based on increasing your stakes to recoup your losses. What we would do is stake more when we are *winning*, stake *less* when we are losing. Therefore, the bank is playing the normal system—and as we know, all normal systems fail. We also have a crucial advantage. When our stakes go up we will be playing with the bank's money—"

"How the hell can one play with the bank's money?"

"Naturally we require capital to start with—but not a great deal. Under the staking system we bet at the minimum stake when we are losing, because that is our own capital. It is theoretically possible we could each go on losing over days, even weeks. In that case we would eventually lose our capital. Probability, however, says that *some* of us would be winning every day. And only when the player starts winning does he increase his stakes. But he never increases them beyond what he has just won. In other words, he is playing with the bank's money."

He shook his head, although his manner seemed less dogmatic. "Surely the zero wheel gives the bank a permanent advantage?"

"Yes, but only of one point four percent on the even chances. Suppose you had a hundred pounds capital, Mr. Blake, what is one point four percent of that? You may lose your hundred pounds but *not* because of the zero percentage."

"I have *seen* people play roulette, you know. They

win, they lose—more frequently the latter in my experience. Surely it is only in trashy films that one sees long winning sequences with the chips piling up? I mean to say—"

"You are talking about *gamblers*, Mr. Blake, hunch players and the like, people chasing dreams. My method involves a dedicated team playing percentages to a scientific staking method. We won't be trying our luck for a couple of hours, you know, we'll be applying ourselves to a rigid pattern for days on end. We will be playing as a team, pooling our capital, covering *all* the even chances, most important of all—pooling our winnings."

"I must say I like the concept," he said grudgingly. "However, it seems too obvious—why has nobody thought of it before?"

"A certain Lord Beresford thought of it in 1926, in principle at least. I came across an old copy of a book he wrote. Others may have tried to put his idea of reversing a system into practice; I don't know. What I really think is that the world is full of diehards calling themselves experts. Has any major scientific discovery not been howled down by established opinion? Yet years later people say, how blindingly obvious, why did nobody think of that before? I must stress that, Mr. Blake. We are trying something *unique*."

"Mmmm." Blake gave himself a few moments to ponder. Then he looked up, almost smiling. "I admit I'm attracted to this idea of forcing the bank to play the system against the player, Mr. Leigh. Its impudence appeals to me. Very well—when do we start?"

"Here is my card. Think it over and then give me a ring. You do understand I'm not offering a Cook's tour? My other teams floundered through stupidity and willfulness. This time the keynote will be hard work. There will be no democratic decisions, no discussions, simply a

blind acceptance of my instructions. You will be trained so rigorously that by the time we go to France everybody in the group will be able to play the Reverse Labouchère as instinctively as breathing. In my experience there is no more *shabby* feeling than that of leaving a casino in defeat. I have no intention of ever again enduring that sort of humiliation."

"I'm not given to suffering defeat easily, Mr. Leigh," he said stiffly. "If I decide—"

"If you do, give me a ring." I rose to show him out. He seemed like an officer and a gentleman, but only time would tell.

Peculiarly enough, the people who lasted the obstacle course best were not those who showed immediate enthusiasm but the passive types who merely listened to what I had to say and then left without showing much reaction at all. Among these was a Mr. Richardson, in his fifties, moustachioed, a bony face not so much sunburnt as turned to leather by a lifetime of colonial service in Afghanistan—or so a romantic imagination led me to conjecture. He came to the first interview with a lady he introduced as his wife, although I had my doubts. She was at least twenty years younger than he, blond, not tall but elegant. She had on a jaunty yachting ensemble, little peaked cap, blue blazer, white trousers.

Richardson listened to me without visible reaction and then asked about the money side of the operation.

"First of all I should make it clear that I will at no stage take any money whatsoever from the group," I said. "There will be an initial training period in this house and then a dummy run in a London casino. For that, each member of the team will supply his own staking capital of ninety pounds. I will take ten percent of all winnings— if there are no winnings, I get nothing. When we go to France each member will be required to bring another

ninety pounds each—plus whatever he or she needs for fares and expenses. Again I will take ten percent of the winnings. I hope to make a great deal of money out of this project, but it won't be from the people who go with me."

"That's all I wished to know."

Fewer than half the original interviewees returned for a second interview. To my surprise little Mrs. Heppenstall, the shy widow from Hastings, was one of them. Thinking I had not made myself clear at our first meeting, I said to her tactfully, "You do realize I'm not offering you a job in the south of France, Mrs. Heppenstall?"

"Oh yes, I know that," she replied. "I've thought about it very seriously, and I would like to come along with you —that's if you think I could be useful."

"We'll be in casinos all day, and there'll be a great deal of involved paperwork—it can be very tiring, you know. If I might ask—what makes you think you'd enjoy an experience of this kind?"

"I've always so much wanted to travel abroad," she said apologetically, her eyes watching me hopefully.

It was a glorious evening in June when cars and taxis began to arrive at our home carrying the chosen thirty-seven for the initial training. Pauline and I had spent the whole day dragging chairs, and any item of furniture that could be used as a chair, into the lounge, a magnificent room, forty-two feet by twenty-one, with French windows, Restoration furniture and cream-coloured wallpaper in a cracked-ice motif.

Apart from one foreigner, Mr. Lee Kuan, a young economics student from Hong Kong, the assembled group was a typical cross-section of middle-class England. At that stage only a few had made any impression on me as individuals—Mrs. Heppenstall, of course, smiling shyly; a

young man called Terry Baker about whom I had certain suspicions, his three references having returned identically worded letters; Oliver Blake, dressed as if he were attending a Palace investiture; and a rather prissy man called Bateson, who was a company bookkeeper and seemed to think that made him an expert on the mathematics of staking. The glamorous Mrs. Richardson was also present, but her husband didn't seem to be with her.

For the rest, there were male filing clerks, female secretaries, business executives, company directors, one or two of "independent means," a pubkeeper and the manager of a cement firm.

They knew very little about me, and it was obvious that they were curious. I might have been more nervous but for three or four large Scotches consumed rapidly before the apprehensive eyes of my wife. There is a terrifying sense of responsibility involved in dragging other people into one's private obsession and I needed the stuff to insulate my nervous system.

"Ladies and gentlemen," I began, when they were all seated in our sizable lounge, "before we go any further I'm afraid that at the risk of boring you I must give you a few words of advice concerning this venture. Once we enter a casino the success or failure of our efforts will depend entirely on how well you have assimilated the lessons I propose to teach you in this room. If we are to make any money, your co-operation and obedience is essential. I am *determined* that once we start we shall not fail. You will be up against this little gadget"—I tapped the spokes of the wheel—"and to beat it you will have to become something not unlike machines yourselves. There must be no deviation from the system I'm going to teach you. All human reason has to be rigorously excluded. You may feel tired, you may at times think it is just not your day, your nerves may well reach breaking point—well, towards

all these excuses you will find me unsympathetic. This is to be a team effort, and my responsibility is to ensure that no individual lets the rest of the team down. To this end you will be disciplined and trained until you can work the system without thinking. If you find the practice sessions here too arduous, you should drop out before we come to play with real money. Contrary to myth, the real stumbling block to success at roulette is neither in the law of averages nor in chance—it is that people are happier losing. They would deny it vehemently, but I've seen it countless times —losing is more comfortable than winning. Winning demands ruthlessness and a willingness to forget all other considerations.

"From the moment you step inside a casino you will be faced with every temptation known to man—drink, sex, greed, egomania, even fear. While you are working you will have to become puritans. I have been careful to stress all along that I guarantee nothing. I'd like you all to think of this as an adventure which offers a reasonable chance of making money, but it will be an adventure we can look back on with satisfaction only if we all pull our weight.

"What I propose to do this evening is run through the basic rules of the system, the Reverse Labouchère. This will give you a taste of what playing method roulette is all about. Some of you may very well feel that such involved paperwork is not your cup of tea—if so, have no hesitation in telling me. Better to be honest with yourselves now than waste your time and mine. Well then, to business. I asked you all to bring notepads. In a straight line down the left-hand side of the page write the numbers one, two, three, four. . . ."

I stopped spinning the wheel at about ten o'clock. Reactions were varied. Some seemed to think it was all too easy and wondered why I was making such a fuss. A few were still frowning at the effort required in taking

their rusty adult minds back to the classroom. Bateson the bookkeeper wanted to ask a number of technical questions.

"One step at a time if you don't mind, Mr. Bateson," I said firmly. "You all have some idea of what the method entails. Is there anyone who would rather drop out now?"

"I'll tell you one thing," said a young Londoner with ginger hair. "It looks a whole lot easier when James Bond's doing it in the movies. I got a headache with them sums."

"I found it easy enough," said Blake.

"Funny, you don't look like James Bond," retorted the ginger-haired man. Blake coloured but said nothing.

"Right," I said. "I'm glad the headaches haven't put anyone off. To save the group's time with the kind of questions you were asking, Mr. Bateson, I've had run off some copies of a leaflet which outlines the fundamental principles of my system. You can each take a copy home and study it before our next get-together. I would ask you not to let anyone else read it."

As they were leaving, Mrs. Richardson came up to me.

"My husband decided it would be easier if I came along instead of him," she said, her voice so hoarse I assumed she had a stiff cold. "Will that be all right?"

"Of course—there's no sex discrimination here, I assure you."

"Will it be all right to show him this?" She held up the stapled sheets of the leaflet I had distributed. "I promise he won't talk about it."

"I was half-joking, actually. It isn't likely that anyone would—"

"You don't want to be too trusting, Mr. Leigh," she said seriously. "There are a lot of sharks about these days."

As I watched the last of them going down the drive to their cars I found myself wondering—was it too much to hope that my obstacle course of interviews and character references had eliminated all the bad eggs? A team

of thirty-seven? I could have *six* shifts, cover *two* tables, double the chances of winning progressions. . . .

As I got into bed Pauline, obviously surprised, remarked that my wild project seemed to have attracted a very decent assortment of people.

"Well, you can't tell at this stage," I said wearily.

"Don't be so cynical. They all seemed totally respectable."

"So did all the other maniacs, at first."

•5

The pamphlet I had given the group to take home explained everything one would need to know in order to
beat the table, the master plan if you like. I reproduce it
here in a slightly shortened form. It was headed:

PRIVATE AND CONFIDENTIAL

As a preliminary, it might be as well to dispose of one or
two misconceptions concerning the game of roulette. In
the first place, nobody ever "beats the bank." The bank
has in its favour zero, which over a period of time appro-
priates 2.1 percent of all monies staked on the table (2.8
percent on numbers and combinations of numbers, and
1.4 percent on even chances). Thus, in effect, the bank
acts as broker, levying its brokerage of 2.1 percent on
winner and loser alike. When a player has a substantial
win he does *not* take it from the bank but from the other
players.

Let us imagine a player who has been playing on even
chances and numbers and has won £1,000, in the process
staking a total of £100. He will have lost to the bank by
way of zero the sum of £2 2s (2.1 percent). The sum he
has won came initially from the other players so that it,
too, was subject to zero.

As a result of these transactions the bank has acquired exactly £23 2s. To the casual eye it might appear that the player has won £1,000 from the bank—yet as we see it is the bank which has actually gained, by taking its percentage of all monies passing across the table. Besides which, over a period of time the player would almost certainly lose his temporary profits and in the meantime all monies staked by him, either to increase these profits or to recover them, would still be subject to the remorseless toll of zero.

The second point is that *all* systems fail in the long run. Every system player knows this, but few realize why. Many, with only a superficial knowledge of the subject, would ascribe this failure to zero. A simple example will prove this false. A hypothetical player with £1,000 capital, playing on even chances and staking flat stakes of £1, would on average lose 3½ pence to zero for every spin of the wheel. Apart from this, of course, his wins and losses will exactly cancel out, and at this rate he will need to stake continually for 72,000 spins before his entire capital is lost, which virtually amounts to an attendance of two hundred days, playing twelve hours a day! Obviously the incidence of zero by itself cannot be held responsible for dramatic changes of fortune.

In point of fact, the really dramatic losses at roulette, especially among system players, can normally be compressed into a very short time, often a matter of hours. Since zero is the only factor (apparently) in the bank's favour, and since its toll of 2.1 percent is negligible as far as the average player is concerned, we are forced to seek elsewhere for the reasons behind "system failure." . . .

[At this point I gave Lord Beresford's account of the "career" of a typical system player using the orthodox Labouchère method of staking, with a capital of £1,000.

It showed that he had to increase his stakes to recover previous losses until an adverse sequence of magnitude takes both his winnings and his capital, the process lasting six days.]

The bank had indeed reaped a rich harvest, for it only needed a capital of £100 (the amount the player won in his first five days), plus a wait of six days, to acquire £1,000. One fact emerges with startling clarity—if the bank itself could be forced to play the system in its *correct* order *against the player* then obviously the tables would be completely turned. This is not as difficult as it sounds. Suppose our hypothetical player, instead of increasing his stakes after a loss and decreasing them after a win, had decreased them after a loss and increased them after a win. The net result would be that instead of setting out to win £20 a day he would actually lose £20 a day and force the bank to take the brunt of the hitherto adverse sequences. It would now be the bank's turn to be content with a paltry £20 a day, coupled with the ever-present danger of an adverse sequence. It would have exactly the same chance (apart from zero) as our player had of continuing to win £20 per day, every day, ad infinitum. The bank would probably succeed in winning £100 over the first five days, only to lose that and its entire capital on the sixth day. It must be remembered that our player has only £1,000 to lose, whereas the bank stands the risk of actually being broken: unlike the player it cannot simply get up and walk away because it has lost £1,000.

The simile is complete except for one small detail. Let us suppose our player had decided to cease play after recovering from the bank his previous losses of £100, plus £1,000 of the bank's capital. In order to win a total of £1,000 on even chances he must have actually staked that amount, although £900 of it actually belonged to

the bank, so that he would still have been subjected to zero—1.4 percent on £1,000. Our player would have won £1,000 less £14, or £986.

[I then outlined the idea of six players covering all the even chances in shifts, staking on the reversed Labouchère method.]

Now, however, *all* six even chances are being played upon simultaneously, so that instead of having to wait an average of six days before the bank is in difficulty any one of the players will on average place the bank in jeopardy at least *once every day*. Not only is the bank forced to play a dangerous system, it is forced to play it against six players at the same time. By way of contrast imagine the folly of a single player attempting to play the Labouchère in its *correct* order against six different tables at the same time (assuming this were physically possible). He would certainly lose his capital on the first day.

To return to our six players, however, we find that within a very short space of time one of them at least has placed the bank in grave difficulties. The other players will continue to lose at a rate of about 100 units per session of four hours. The one who hits a favourable progression will increase his stakes, and since he will be playing with the bank's capital (i.e. his winnings) the size of his stakes will not worry him. Unlike the player using the system in its orthodox order, he can sit there and wait. He does not have to wait very long, for quite suddenly one of two things has happened.

A) His stakes have reached such gigantic proportions that he is barred from staking upwards by reason of the table limit (generally the equivalent of £200 for a single bet on the even chances). At this stage his probable winnings are in the region of £2,000. Now he either terminates his staking on that progression and returns to the basic units, or he is relieved.

B) The size of his stakes has not reached the bank's

limits, presumably because the progression is a longer and more gradual one; the alternatives here are either a collapse of the favourable sequence or breaking the bank. Should the latter be the case he will again either return to normal staking or be relieved. His win here is likely to be in the order of £5,000, which is roughly the capitalization of a roulette table.

Breaking the bank, of course, does not mean that the casino has lost all its available capital, merely that the table concerned has lost all its available chips and plaques and that reserves will have to be brought up from other tables.

The foregoing, it will be obvious, is beyond the scope of the individual operator. In many clubs and casinos the tables are open round the clock and the individual would require relief players—even then he would be covering only a single chance.

[I then described the staking system, Labouchère's starting line of 1, 2, 3, 4, explaining that in its orthodox form it is extremely dangerous because the stakes become so vast, to recoup losses, that they are out of all proportion to the comparatively small amounts won.]

Concerning capital requirements, the interesting thing is that as no player will be working for more than four hours a day (roughly 120 spins) and since the maximum possible loss is 80 percent of the total number of spins (i.e. 96 units) the theoretical requirement for each day will be roughly £12. In practice, however, each player will be required to have available for his own use at least £90.

The player will often find a favourable sequence building up only to see it collapse—this is, indeed, the rule rather than the exception. This can be disheartening, but remember that the bank has exactly the same experience when the method is being used in its correct order against it—but the bank never becomes disheartened. Why

should it? Like ourselves it has but to wait; its croupiers probably work for more than four hours a day so that from the standpoint of mental and physical stamina alone we will have the edge on them. The keynote to the whole operation is diligence and attention to detail.

Players should experience little difficulty in maintaining the simple calculations of the Reverse Labouchère and staking at the same time, since the average interval between spins is about one minute, although it can vary between thirty seconds and as much as three minutes.

Since zero is the only attribute to the bank that we cannot duplicate, its treatment deserves mention. When the ball lands in zero one of two things happens to monies staked on even chances; the player's stake is imprisoned and he may *partager,* that is remove one half of it, leaving the other half to the bank, or he can leave it on for its fate to be decided by the next spin. Thus if he bets on red and zero comes up, his stake would be imprisoned. If black comes up next he loses the whole stake. If red comes up he recovers it in its entirety (although he does not *win* any money). Either way the result over a long period is the same: 1.4 percent to the bank.

In practice players should leave the stake in "prison," treat zero as if it had not occurred, and place their stakes on the selected chance a second time, taking care, however, to recover their previous stake in the event of its being released from prison.

Finally, the golden rule: never allow yourself to be flustered; never take part in other people's disputes—you are there to make money, they are probably only there for a flutter—and strive at all times to keep up with the wheel.

TO THE READER:

My group had the advantage of applying the lessons set out in my pamphlet in many hours of practice in my home

at Twickenham, and even then some of them were slow to assimilate everything. Do not despair, therefore, if you fail to grasp all the subtleties of roulette after one reading. If, however, you feel you've grasped the principle, there is one thing I must stress.

This is, indeed, a system for winning at roulette, but before anyone packs in his job and mortgages his house to rush to the nearest casino with his life savings I must state categorically—it is not easy money. It needs a carefully selected team, a great deal of practice, physical stamina and a fairly stern frame of mind. That still leaves yo with the conditions of a casino to contend with. And as w were to discover, nobody is going to let you win big 1 oney without putting up a fight, dirty or otherwise.

·6

The roulette academy, as the group took to calling our practice sessions, lasted for five weeks from May to June, 1966, probably the first and only roulette school—for players, not croupiers—in this country. People came and went in streams. Every night of the week and all day on the weekends I stood behind the table, spinning the wheel, throwing the ball, calling the stock phrases. As most were learning roulette from scratch they had to be taught the basic French vocabulary and the elementary rules before they could be drilled in the mathematics of the Reverse Labouchère. Occasionally we would break off for a drink to give their brains a rest from figure work, but even then I discouraged conversation on any topic but roulette.

A rather retiring man called Nathan asked at one break: "How can you tell who is a mug in this game and who isn't? I mean, how do we know we won't be mugs as well?"

"By *mug* I mean someone who lets the casino take his money and doesn't care because he gets a kick out of playing the big shot," I said. "He's always well dressed, generally drinks a lot and almost invariably has a good-looking female in tow. He's very popular with the table

staff—naturally, he always shows how important he is by chucking them a big tip."

"Do we tip the croupier?" asked Mrs. Richardson.

"I object to tipping them in principle," I said. "However, from a practical point of view it's advisable to give them something or they'll start messing you about, pretending not to hear you when you want to change a high-denomination plaque for chips, that sort of thing. Give them no more than two or three pounds at the end of your session. By the way, the croupier is the one who has the stick and rakes in the chips—the one who spins the wheel is the tourneur. Then there's the Chef de Partie—he's there to supervise the table and he also acts as a sort of umpire if there are any disputes."

"You mentioned drinking," said a burly man called Milton. "Do you object to us having the odd drink while we're playing?"

I smiled. "Mr. Milton, I am not running a temperance campaign. I object to nothing—provided it in no way impairs your ability to play the system. Some people can drink and remain sensible, a lot more only *think* they can. That's the danger, but basically it's up to the individual. If you're asking my advice, I'd say stick to coffee. A roulette salon is a peculiar environment, you know. It brings out strange elements in the personality. Shy people can become showoffs, cautious people can turn into maniacs. It's often hard to remember that you're actually dealing in hard cash—that's why chips were invented in the first place, to delude players into forgetting that they're betting in real money."

"Surely casinos make money anyway, though, without having to rely on a lot of tricks and gimmicks?" somebody asked.

"No?" I said. "The whole thing is a psychological gimmick. The first thing you'll notice is the atmosphere

—it won't be like the poker school in Dodge City. It's deliberately contrived to be formal and somber to over-awe the player. They're implanting in the clientele the idea that here is the utmost respectability—what could you possibly have to worry about? The truth is that casinos attract an undesirable element. The sophisticated and beautiful young lady giving you a charming smile is less likely to be a debutante than a harpy looking for a winner to fleece. Those ultrapolite croupiers, so helpful and co-operative? Yes, when you are losing. Start winning seriously and that tugging you feel at your feet is the red carpet being brutally pulled from under you. The great thing is to speak to nobody, to trust nobody. For instance, whenever possible keep your high-denomination chips and plaques out of sight in a handbag or pocket. Leave only the low-denomination chips on the table in front of you."

"Why—would anybody seriously try to steal chips from under your nose?" asked Blake incredulously.

"There are people who make a living by doing simply that," I answered. "Look, I'll show you."

I put a pile of the plastic chips on the table and asked Blake to take the chair. I stood at his left shoulder.

"You are very busy," I said. "You're watching the wheel, you're doing your calculations and selecting chips and plaques for your next stake. I'm one of the thirty or forty people standing round the table behind the few who have seats. I go to place my own bet—so." My arm stretched across him and as my wrist passed over his chips I let my shirt cuff cut the top two or three chips off his pile. They fell off the pile on to the cloth. "Now, if I had the professional thief's razor-sharp cuffs, those chips would have disappeared up my sleeve," I said. "Would you have noticed? Twenty or thirty pounds of your capital has gone. It's quite common—in France they usually get seven or eight years' jail if they're caught."

After that particular session I was seeing them off at the front door when I saw Mrs. Richardson giving me a curious look.

"Well, Mrs. Richardson," I said, "how does your husband feel about all this, you being out every night?"

"Oh, he gives me plenty of rope. He would have liked to come himself but he has his job."

"Let me guess—army, I should say. Brigadier, perhaps?"

She frowned and laughed at the same time. "Brigadier? That's very funny. I must tell him. Anyway, when we realized you were serious about going to France we decided I could best be spared from the domestic front —our three boys are all at boarding school and George— the Brigadier!—said I could have a little break. He's a better cook than I am in any case."

"Three sons?" I said. "If I may say so—"

"Oh *don't*. Everyone does, it gets so boring to be always hearing tributes to one's fecundity," she said in her perpetually hoarse voice. "I say it to myself enough, I *am* too young to have three sons at boarding school. Between you and me, that's why the Brigadier gives me plenty of rope. I was a child bride!"

What could I say to that?

As she was stepping out into the porch one of the men, Peter Vincent, a languid, rather too handsome young man, came back up the drive.

"Care for a lift?" he asked Mrs. Richardson.

She turned back to me, apparently giving him the cold shoulder. "Just one point—I've always been good at maths, but some of them feel you're a bit impatient: you expect them to grasp everything at first telling."

"I'll watch that. Good night."

As she walked away, I heard her accept Vincent's offer of a lift: "Only snag is that I doubt your boot is big enough to give my car a lift as well."

Pauline could see I was impressed by Mrs. Richardson, but she restrained herself from comment. Not once had she complained during these weeks when our house seemed like Waterloo Station, with streams of people taking over her lounge for nonstop roulette sessions. Her tolerance was all the more praiseworthy considering that she didn't have a great deal of faith in this grandiose scheme of mine; but not once did she nag at me to give it up. Far from it, she even volunteered to act as a permanent reserve when we began to play in the Regency. I'd been explaining to her that I was playing a trick on the team by drumming into them the absolute necessity of staking on every single spin of the wheel.

"But they'll need to go to the toilet, won't they?" she asked.

"I'll be there at all times."

"What if two want to go at once?"

"Look, it doesn't really matter a jot if they miss a spin or two, it's only a psychological gambit on my part —tell them every spin is vital and they stay keyed up. Creative tension. They've only got a minute or so between spins, they've got to calculate the next stake, select the chips and get the bet on. If I tell them it makes no difference to the system to miss the odd spin for a trip to the lavatory, they'll start taking little rests when they feel like it. The smallest break in concentration is enough to cause a mental blockage. I've got them believing that total continuity is a kind of magic spell: if it breaks, the whole system collapses. They're going to discipline themselves, and that's the only discipline you can rely on."

"All the more reason for having me there," she said firmly.

I instigated phase two after three weeks of practice in my lounge.

"I want you all to have enrolled as members of the Regency by next Wednesday," I said. "You can go there on your own or in twos or threes—but no more than that. The longer we disguise the group from the club's management the better. Just walk through the front door and tell the receptionist you want to join. You should be proposed for membership by an existing member, but they'll soon find somebody to sponsor you. Then you just pay your thirty shillings [$4.20] and collect your card. Once you've all been infiltrated we start playing in earnest."

"Why all the secrecy?" demanded, as I might have guessed, the pedantic Mr. Bateson.

"Don't worry, we're not breaking the law," I told him. "We want simply to avoid the sensation that a phalanx of thirty-seven roulette players would cause marching in as a body."

The date set was June 13. By June 11 all thirty-seven had their membership cards. On the evening of June 12 we had our final meeting at my home. I handed round sheets of paper with the shift allocations and which of the six even-chance bets each member of the group would be covering. Then I gave them the final briefing.

"We start work seriously tomorrow at three," I said. "I think I've managed to fit everybody into a shift that will suit him. The first group of twelve must be in the casino promptly at two forty-five to make sure they get seats. We will occupy two roulette tables, entering the club in small groups. We will not speak to each other except in an emergency, when I will be there to help you. As individuals you must not dress conspicuously or draw attention to yourselves in any way. You will each have your day's staking capital of ten pounds [$28]. If anything untoward happens, you will behave with the utmost formality. Remember—once we start winning the casino boys will be watching like hawks for some excuse to bar

us from the club. You must not drink to excess nor allow yourself to be picked up by any of the good-time girls. The first shift will play from three until seven. You will not leave your seat until your replacement is actually standing at your shoulder; otherwise someone else could grab the chair. You will leave any loose chips or plaques in front of your place when you vacate your seat. The second shift should be in the casino by six forty-five and will take up the staking exactly where the first shift left off. The third shift will be present in the casino at ten forty-five when the same procedure will be followed. At all times my wife or myself will be available to take over the chair of anyone who wishes to use the lavatory. If for any reason you can't make one of your allocated sessions you must phone me here as quickly as possible so that I can arrange a cover for you. I should hope this would happen only in a genuine emergency. You have all reached the stage where you can work the system with ease—let us now see if you can work it under real conditions. Remember the three main dangers—drink, women and conversation. Stick to the system, don't miss a single spin, ignore all distractions and you will not need luck. Are there any questions?"

"All we need is Jack Hawkins to tell us the target," drawled the handsome Peter Vincent. The laughter was too loud for what the joke merited, a clear indication of the general tension.

Oliver Blake gave Vincent a severe glare. "Mr. Leigh," he said stiffly, "I think I speak for everyone here when I say how much we appreciate the hard work you've invested in this venture. I for one have no intention of letting you or the team down by treating it in a casual manner."

This was met with murmurs of agreement. Vincent shrugged.

"Mr. Vincent, that's a fine bit of cloth you're wearing,"

I commented. "What will your reaction be tomorrow if in the middle of a progression some half-drunk oaf standing behind you rams the lighted end of a cigar into your back?"

Vincent smiled about the eyes but kept a straight face.

"I'll carry on staking, of course. Have no fear, Mr. Leigh, I'm learning something about the Eton code."

The portly Blake pretended not to hear Vincent's jibe.

7

The fifteen graduates of the roulette academy who infiltrated the Regency that sunny June afternoon—the first
shift of twelve plus three whose freedom from economic
bondage enabled them to come along out of curiosity—
were not a happy bunch of fun-loving friends. One or
two had struck up mild liaisons, several of the men showed
willingness to get on closer terms with Mrs. Richardson,
but basically they were strangers who had nothing in
common but a strong desire to make money. Not that I
held greed against anybody—I was *praying* I might at last
have found people who were truly hungry for cash rather
than less profitable pleasures. Yet I found myself thinking
nostalgically of earlier episodes in France with aristocratic
drunks and irrepressible eccentrics. This current bunch
seemed stuffy and dull by comparison. Still, I had chosen
them for these very qualities, and success meant more to
me than personal amusement.

That first day nothing happened. Nothing. Nobody
succeeded in reaching the table's limit or breaking the
bank. Rogers had the first whiff of a progression on black
but when his stakes had reached £30 or £40 (about
$85 to $110), red began to predominate and soon he had
crossed out all the figures on his line, meaning of course

that he had lost his original investment of 10 shillings.

The combined losses for the day came to £110, each of the thirty-six who actually played having staked only a percentage of the £10 I had told them to bring for each session.

It was about ten minutes to four on the afternoon of our second day that we had our first smell of action. It happened to Sydney Hopplewell, a company director of around sixty, a white-haired man who during the weeks of training had always been reserved to the point of rudeness.

"What the hell does he think he's doing?" I muttered to Pauline as I saw Hopplewell getting up from his chair, his place being taken by a middle-aged woman. Moving quickly between the tables, I came up beside Hopplewell to issue my first rebuke. His last bet on *impair*, odd, had just won. I waited while he picked up his chips and wrote in his notebook. To my surprise I saw that he had started a progression. *Impair* was coming up in a predominance of 5 to 2. His stakes rose quickly.

Saying nothing that might divert his attention, I stood at his elbow, ready to give assistance. He was a portly figure with a complexion not so much highly coloured as congested. Jostled on all sides, having to hold his notepad in his hand, trying to keep track of the chips and plaques being shoved at him by the croupier, he started to sweat profusely. His stakes reached £14 and then £16. I held my breath; was this it, our first winning progression?

He cracked up without warning. Before I could stop him he drew a shaky pencil line through his row of three-digit figures, turned to a new page and wrote 1, 2, 3, 4.

His first stake of 5 shillings lost. So did the next. The favourable run of *impair* had petered out.

Nothing else happened that second day. After the casino closed in the early hours a dozen or so of the

group came back to Twickenham for a chat. Hopplewell was so embarrassed he could not speak, though nobody but myself had noticed that he had had the start of a progression. I could have kept quiet, but the purpose of playing the Regency was to drill these people into a reliable team, not mollycoddle the sensitive. After I had offered everyone a drink I turned to him and said, "Well, Mr. Hopplewell?"

With a face like his it was impossible to detect a blush. Gruffly he said, in a louder voice than usual: "I'm terribly sorry. I had a progression under way this afternoon and I fluffed it."

"What do you mean *fluffed it*?" Rogers demanded aggressively.

"I was staking in hundreds of units and then I lost concentration—I just couldn't think. I went back to five shillings."

"Jesus Christ!" snapped Rogers, expecting me to launch a tirade.

"It wasn't quite as simple as that, Mr. Hopplewell," I said, neither aggressively nor sympathetically. "Why did you stand up?"

"There was a lady standing behind me, an American. I heard her saying she felt a bit giddy, so I gave her my seat," he explained.

"Of all the stupid bloody—"

"You were too much of a gentleman, Mr. Hopplewell," I said. "I'm afraid good manners don't win money in a casino. I would hate to be responsible for advocating a further deterioration in public behaviour, but your sense of etiquette might very well have cost us two or three thousand pounds."

"You were bloody told about getting hold of the seats and sticking to them," Rogers ranted.

Then Blake stepped in. "None of us is so perfect that we can criticize at this stage," he said authoritatively.

"I just didn't think," said Hopplewell. "I am very sorry."

"Don't feel too bad about it," I said, prepared to be sympathetic now that I saw the lesson had gone home. Hopplewell did not seem the type to apologize easily. "It was the first progression any of you has had to deal with, and it's precisely to obviate such mistakes that we're playing in real conditions before we go to France. That woman probably tricked you deliberately, Mr. Hopplewell. She could not have been standing for very long, and it wasn't particularly hot in the salon that early in the afternoon."

"Dear oh dear, you just can't trust nobody these days," joked Robinson, the ginger-haired young clerk, a joke that was to have greater point at a later stage.

This incident helped the whole team—and certainly had a deep effect on Hopplewell. At his first interview he had told me bluntly he despised all forms of gambling as catering to adolescent minds. My explanation of the scheme had decided him that for the small amount of capital involved it might be worth a short dabble—purely as a business speculation, he said. He was one of the group most likely to drop out at any excuse I would have said but the tantalizing nearness of £2,000 ($5,600) on only our second day proved to be exactly the right psychological carrot. Mr. Hopplewell had made his last mistake.

Pandemonium broke loose in the Regency at precisely 7:12 the following evening, our third day in the casino. I remember the time so precisely because the second shift had just taken over the seats and I had just come back upstairs from seeing Pauline off home in a taxi. I had a stroll round the two tables where our second shift of

twelve was settling down for four hours' solid roulette. Seeing that Mrs. Richardson's stakes were moving up slightly, I stood behind her. The casino was not particularly busy, the afternoon crowd having drifted off and the late-nighters not yet emerging from restaurants and theaters. There were possibly a dozen people standing round that table.

From her notepad I could see that Mrs. Richardson had already played four spins. She was betting in units of 1 shilling (14 cents), on *pair*, the even numbers.

This is what happened, spin by spin, stake by stake. As always she had taken a clean page and written that familiar line, 1, 2, 3, 4.

Spin 1. She had staked 5 units (5 shillings—one 5-shilling chip). *Pair* came up, so she won 5 shillings and got her stake back. She added the amount of the win to her line, which then read 1, 2, 3, 4, 5. Her next stake was, therefore, 1 + 5—6.

Spin 2. Pair came up again. Having won 6 units, she added that figure to the line, which now read 1, 2, 3, 4, 5, 6. Her next stake was, therefore, 7 units.

Spin 3. She lost. She scored off the figures at either end of the line, which now read 1, 2, 3, 4, 5, 6. She still had to add the figures at either end, so her next stake was 2 + 5—7.

Spin 4. She lost again, making her line read 1, 2, 3, 4, 5, 6. There were only two figures left, so her next stake was 3 + 4—7. If she had lost again, her whole line would have been deleted and she would have restarted with a 5-unit stake. However . . .

Spin 5. Pair came up. Having won, she added the amount of the last stake to the line, which on her pad now looked like 1, 2, 3, 4, 5, 6, 7. As the end figures were now 3 and 7 her next stake was 10 units.

Spin 6. Pair came up again. She added 10 to the line,

which became 1, 2, 3, 4, 5, 6, 7, 10. Her next stake was, therefore, 3 + 10—13.

Spin 7. She lost. Scoring out the end numbers the line was now 1, 2, 3, 4, 5, 6, 7, 10. This reduced her next stake to 11 units and also put her back in the position where another loss would have ended the sequence, taking her back to a fresh start with 1, 2, 3, 4.

In this way her stake gradually increased from 5 units to 11 units, the brakes going on when she started losing. Scoring out the figures at either end of the line when losing ensures that in the event of a prolonged losing sequence, the line would have quickly been deleted altogether, preventing the player from losing a succession of large stakes while chasing previous losses. That is the whole point of reverting to 1, 2, 3, 4. It is not a numerical abracadabra but merely a dead-man's-handle to ensure that, in Mrs. Richardson's case, even if she had gone on losing all day, she would never have been down more than 10 units (10 shillings—$1.40) on any sequence.

At this level of staking, Mrs. Richardson's activities interested nobody else at the table. Waiters came and went with drinks and coffee. Other players were placing much larger bets on single numbers or combinations, some winning, more losing. The low murmur of voices, the clicking of plastic chips on the croupier's stick and the delicate rattling of the ball provided a constant background of noise that was almost reassuringly monotonous.

Spin 14. The stake was now 39 units, and she lost. Her line read 11, 18, 25, making her next stake 11 + 25—36.

Spin 15. Pair came up. She had won 36 units and the line became 11, 18, 25, 36. Next stake—47 units.

Spin 16. She lost. After the end numbers had been scored out the line became 18, 25. Next stake—43 units.

Spin 17. She won. The line became 18, 25, 43. (Wins rapidly increase the stake once the smaller opening figures

have been deleted.) Mrs. Richardson's next stake was 61 units.

Spin 18. She won. The line was now 18, 25, 43, 61. Her next stake: 79 units.

Spin 19. She won again. The line became 18, 25, 43, 61, 79. Her next stake was 97 units.

Spin 20. Pair came up again. Mrs. Richardson was well into the progression by now. Her line was 18, 25, 43, 61, 79, 97. Her next stake was 18 + 97—115 units (£5 15s —$16). By this stage the croupiers were beginning to show interest as they saw a staking pattern emerging, but her bets were not yet dramatic enough to alert the other people at the table.

Spin 30. She had been playing for roughly an hour. Her stake was 413 units. Having started with a 5-shilling stake, everything she was now betting had been won *from the bank.* This time she lost. The line was reduced to two figures, 146, 235. These had both been winning bets originally; added together they showed her current winnings less the 10 units represented by the starting line 1, 2, 3, 4.

Her next stake was 381. If she had lost, her winnings would have been wiped out and she would have lost her capital of 10 units for the sequence.

Spin 31. Pair came up. The line became 146, 235, 381. Her next stake was 527 units.

The difference in the atmosphere was marked now. Waiters could hardly take orders for drinks or coffee for trying to watch the woman who was piling up the chips and plaques. Youngish, attractive women are not generally expected to play roulette with professional skill. Mrs. Richardson had had her blond hair restyled with those honey-coloured streaks. In deference to my instruction that the team should dress inconspicuously, she was wearing a black cocktail dress, but the simplicity of its lines only underlined her attractiveness.

Blake had turned up by then, although he was not due to play until the third shift took over at eleven. "You've come just in time to see some action," I said, nodding in the direction of Mrs. Richardson. Blake surveyed the table for a few minutes, looking every inch a City gent who had wandered into something sleazy by mistake.

"She's certainly attracting a great deal of attention," he said. "You warned us against that."

"There's no way you can hide a long winning streak, not when the player is relentlessly upping the stakes."

"Certainly not when the player looks like Mrs. Richardson."

Spin 32. Pair came up, giving her a win of £26 7s ($73). Her line became 146, 235, 381, 527. Her next stake was 673 units.

Spin 33. She lost and had to score out the end numbers, which gave her a line of 235, 381. Adding these, she next staked 616 units.

Spin 34. Pair came up. The line became 235, 381, 616. She selected plaques and chips for 851 units from the piles in front of her. One or two players were trying to latch onto her luck by now, and as soon as she placed her handful of plaques and chips on the rectangle marked *pair* other hands shot out to place stakes beside hers. Of course, they thought it was luck—if they had been following her betting from the start they would have known that she never bet on anything but *pair*.

Spin 35. Pair came up! The croupier pushed plaques and chips worth £42 11s ($119) across the green baize. Mrs. Richardson had time only to push them among the stuff piled loosely in front of her. She wrote the winning stake at the end of the line, which now read 235, 381, 616, 851. Her next stake was 1,086 units.

Spin 36. She won again. Other players tried to get a glimpse of her notepad, but all they could see was a neat

mass of figures, many of them crossed out. Her line was now 235, 381, 616, 851, 1,086. Her next stake was 1,321 units—

Spin 37. Pair! She won 1,321 units and put that figure at the end of her line, which was now 235, 381, 616, 851, 1,086, 1,321. Smiling, she picked out plaques and chips for 1556 units.

Spin 38. Pair again. Her line was now 235, 381, 616, 851, 1,086, 1,321, 1,556. Her next stake was 235 + 1,556— 1,791 units.

Spin 39. She won again! Her line was now 235, 381, 616, 851, 1,086, 1,321, 1,556, 1,791. Her next stake: 235 + 1,791—2,026. She was over the £100 mark and currently winning 7,837 shillings ($1,100).

Spin 40. Another win. Her line became 235, 381, 616, 851, 1,086, 1,321, 1,556, 1,791, 2,026. Other players stared at her in disbelief. A roulette table is a place where small amounts of money change hands quickly in the normal way of things, the whole thing being so geared that no one bet can win more than approximately £200 ($560). This staking pattern, however, was giving her a whole run of bets at less than the table maximum—and her accumulated winnings were beginning to look extremely impressive. Her next stake was 235 + 2,026—2,261.

Spin 41. She won again! The atmosphere round the table was electric. Everybody present was watching every move she made. She selected chips to make up a stake of 2,496 units. She was so quick with her calculations she had time to look up and give Blake and myself a grimace of amusement. *"Rien ne va plus,"* called the tourneur. The clicking of the ball as it circled the rim of the wheel was the only sound I could hear.

Spin 42. She won again. Her line was now 235, 381, 616, 851, 1,086, 1,321, 1,556, 1,791, 2,026, 2,261, 2,496. Her next stake was 235 + 2,496—2,731.

Spin 43. Pair! "By jove, she's done it again. She can't lose!" exclaimed Blake. It was the first time I had seen him so excited, but I said nothing. A fat man in a blue corduroy suit seemed on the point of asking Mrs. Richardson what system she was using. Her line was now 235, 381, 616, 851, 1,086, 1,321, 1,556, 1,791, 2,026, 2,261, 2,496, 2,731. Her next stake was 235 + 2,731—2,966.

Spin 44. She lost. Other players watched her face but saw no sign of disappointment. Why should she have been upset? She had started with a stake of 5 shillings, after all, so the bank had merely won some of its money back. She crossed out the end figures on her line and put down her next stake—381 + 2,496—2,877. The strain on her now was enormous and the slightest interference might have blown her up. The fat man chewed his cheek. I started to move in close to shield her. He said something before I could intervene. She ignored him completely! The fat man frowned but didn't persist. I took a deep breath.

"Good God, I had no idea it would be this nerve-wracking!" said Blake.

Spin 45. She won. Her line was now 381, 616, 851, 1,086, 1,321, 1,556, 1,791, 2,026, 2,261, 2,496, 2,877. Her next stake was therefore 381 + 2,877—3,258.

Spin 46. She won again and added her last stake to the end of the line. Her next stake would be 381 + 3,258—3,639. We were getting near the crucial test now. The maximum possible bet was £200 or 4,000 units ($560). How well would she remember all that I had taught her?

Spin 47. Pair. She had won—but did she know it was for the last time? I had already added the end figures of her line, and her stake would have been 4,020 units, above the staking limit. If she had tried to stake above the limit, the croupier would have politely refused the bet, his eye so well trained he could tell at a glance the value of a pile of plaques and chips. No great harm would

have been done—unless she had decided to go on with stakes just below the maximum. That's what a gambler would do in the middle of a favourable progression like that. The whole success of the system depends on an upward *progression* of stakes when you are winning. To bet on at the ceiling without being able to increase the stakes gives the mathematical advantage straight back to the bank.

Blake was going to say something, but I pushed at his arm to keep him quiet. The tourneur made his call: *"Faites vos jeux."*

Mrs. Richardson glanced again at her pad and frowned. She looked up and caught my eye. I nodded. She smiled, scored out her whole line and ripped that page off her pad. On a new sheet she wrote 1, 2, 3, 4, the gold wedding ring on her left hand shining dully under the lights. With delicate, precise movements, she picked out a 5-shilling chip and almost disdainfully placed it on the space marked *pair*.

"Perfect," I exclaimed to Blake.

"How much has she won?" he asked incredulously.

"That's easy to tell," I said. I leaned over and picked up the last sheet she had torn off her notepad, at the same time murmuring to her, "Not bad for a first attempt."

I showed Blake her page. "You see these figures she scored off at the end, the ones with the vertical line through them? Those are the ones she had left when she reached the limit. All you have to do is add them and that's what she's won."

We needed a pen to work it out. The line was 381, 616, 851, 1,086, 1,321, 1,556, 1,791, 2,026, 2,261, 2,496, 2,877, 3,258, 3,639. It adds up to 24,159 units. The units are, of course, shillings. She had won £1,207 19s (about $3,400).

"Incredible," said Blake. Mrs. Richardson lit a cigarette and blew smoke up towards the lights. She smiled serenely at the croupiers. The ball was already running round the rim of the wheel. Our first winning progression, and she had handled it beautifully!

Later she told us: "It all seemed to happen so quickly. After only a few spins I knew I was winning. I said to myself, 'This is it!' The instant rush of activity literally drove everything else out of my head. I think *pair* (even numbers) was coming up about three times more often than *impair* (odd numbers). Within about twenty spins I was betting what seemed like an awful lot of chips, but I'd forgotten by then it was real money, totally forgotten! My stakes kept getting bigger and bigger—I couldn't keep track of what the man was shoving at me across the table. I remembered you telling us to put the large-denomination plaques out of sight in my handbag but I didn't have time. It just seemed to be running away with me. Then I realized I was getting near the limit. I kept thinking—you have to score out all these figures and start with one, two, three, four again. I was sure I was going to make a mistake and I couldn't remember what would happen if you tried to be above the limit. It was a fantastic experience."

"I'm sorry I couldn't stop that man from speaking to you," I said.

"What man? I didn't hear anybody speaking to me."

It was then about half-past eight. Puzzled by her decision not to make the most of this phenomenally lucky streak, the other players gradually lost interest in Mrs. Richardson. The atmosphere began to return to normal.

I was thinking of going to the bar for a whisky with Blake when Mrs. Heppenstall, the apologetic little widow

from Hastings, began to get a few wins on whatever chance she had been allocated, black if my memory is correct. It had seemed brave of her even to enter such an unlikely place as a gambling club (the nearest she had been to organized gaming before were church whist drives), but to see her small, grey head bent over her notepad and her small, white hand shoving on the chips was unbelievably incongruous.

"I'd better stay and watch her," I said to Blake. "I'm sure she doesn't really grasp what this is all about."

As Mrs. Richardson had just proved—and remember, that had been my first experience of a Reverse Labouchère progression under real conditions as well—a prolonged winning streak puts the player under a very harsh spotlight. The sheer weight of attention can be quite terrifying. As I was standing at Mrs. Heppenstall's shoulder Vincent appeared beside me. Looking at my watch, I saw that it was just after nine. He was not due to take over with the third shift until eleven. When he saw that she was staking something like £60 ($170), he turned to me and said quietly, "Inspiring, isn't it, an old dear like her playing with the big boys?"

"I've seen so-called big boys crack up under less strain than she's going through," I replied.

Vincent, who carried himself in such a lounging manner one was always surprised to realize just how big he was close up, gave me a little nod, the half-smile about his eyes seeming to indicate that he could see through me. "You get your kicks this way, do you, corrupting innocent old ladies?"

"I'm under the impression I am running a serious gaming coup," I said. "How do you get your kicks?" He shook his head imperceptibly, his mocking eyes telling me I would have to do better than that to needle him.

Mrs. Heppenstall's progression was a long one. It had

started with a lot of winning bets, which meant that her line of figures remained on the small side, producing stakes that edged up much more slowly than Mrs. Richardson's. It wasn't until about ten minutes to eleven that she reached four-digit figures. When Vincent came back from the bar I told him to let her see the progression out. He shrugged, apparently finding the whole thing rather childish. The third shift took over at eleven, the switching of seats taking place without incident, happening with such quick precision none of the other players standing round the table had a chance to grab any of the chairs.

At fifteen minutes past eleven Mrs. Heppenstall drew a neat line through her long list of uncrossed figures, wrote 1, 2, 3, 4 on a clean page and prepared to place a stake of 5 shillings.

"It's after eleven," I whispered in her ear. "Mr. Vincent will take over now. Leave all that loose stuff on the table."

I went with her to the cash desk to pay in the large-denomination plaques she had put in her handbag. Mrs. Richardson was waiting for us. When the cashier had counted out the last 10-pound note I turned to them both with a smile.

"You won a great deal of money there, Mrs. Heppenstall," I said. "Over two thousand pounds with what you left on the table. You won one thousand two hundred and seven pounds, Mrs. Richardson. I think that calls for a drink, don't you?"

"Oh, no, I must hurry or I'll miss my train," said Mrs. Heppenstall. I went down with her to the front entrance. "Will I get a bus to Victoria Station at this time of night?" she asked.

"Treat yourself to a taxi, Mrs. Heppenstall. After all— two thousand pounds!"

"Perhaps I will, just this once." We went out onto the

pavement. As I watched for a cab she said, sounding worried, "It's an awful lot of money, isn't it? Are you sure it's all right?"

Thinking she meant the cab fare, I said I would give her £10. "We'll have a proper share-out when I've had time to work out the amounts. The taxi won't be more than a pound."

"Actually I meant"—she looked nervously back into the club's brilliantly lit foyer—"I only started with ten pounds. Are you sure it's all right—taking all that much from them?"

"All right?" I looked at her small, country-fresh face to see if this were a joke. It was not. "Of course it's all right—that's what it's all *for*. Didn't you realize we could win that much?"

"Well, not really—I'm terribly afraid what we're doing is illegal. Are you sure we—"

"My dear lady, don't worry. I wouldn't drag you into anything even remotely shady. That's what gambling means—you bet your money against theirs. If you win you take it all away with you. If you'd lost, they wouldn't be shedding any tears over you, believe me."

I watched her go off in a taxi and went back upstairs, where Mrs. Richardson was having a martini at the bar.

"Incredible—she didn't realize we kept the money! I I think she was under the impression this is merely a ritual that goes on in here and that people do it just for the amusement!"

"That's probably why she sailed through her progression so calmly—just imagine what a state she would have been in if she'd thought she was staking hundreds of pounds for real!"

"That's the whole point of playing here, to get everybody acclimatized."

"I'll tell you one thing," she said, lighting a cigarette. "The greasy boys are watching us like hawks now."

"The greasy boys?"

"The croupiers and the rest of them."

"Very apt. You certainly haven't taken long to acclimatize yourself to the cynical world of casinos."

"Talking about cynics, that man Rogers hasn't turned up, has he?"

"I haven't seen him. Just as well we have one spare member. I wondered if he phoned my house."

"I don't think you'll be seeing him again. I was naive enough to lend him his staking money yesterday—he said he didn't have time to get to the bank. I suppose he decided to forget the whole idea after two days of winning nothing."

"Yes, that was a bit silly of you. Still, better to make that kind of mistake now. Care for another drink?"

"Thank you but no. I must get home and tend to the Brigadier's needs."

"Well, you did extremely well, Mrs. Richardson. You handled our very first progression beautifully."

"I've always been very good at figures. By the way, you could call me Emma—unless you follow your fat friend in such matters."

"Blake? Don't you like him?"

"Since you ask—no."

"Would you say he's honest?"

"Probably."

"I notice that quite a lot of the group take note of what he says."

"All the little snobs looking up to that Eton bullshit."

"Perhaps. I think I might make him our treasurer. That would remove any final doubt that I'm running some complicated form of fraud."

Grinding out the fifth or sixth cigarette she had smoked in those few minutes at the bar, she patted at her honey-streaked hair and said, "That should suit him. His type is well used to handling money that somebody else made."

She left to go home to Pimlico. I went back to the roulette salon. The fact that we had now won over £3,000 ($8,400) had left me feeling not so much elated as relieved. On a venture like this three consecutive days of nonstop losing, however small the sums, might have been enough to start the group breaking up.

Unbelievably I found myself watching our third progression of the day. It happened to Terry Baker, the sales representative whose three identically worded character references had made me suspect he was using a false name for some reason. Not that he was necessarily a crook—quite a number of the people I had interviewed had said they couldn't afford to be associated with casinos and gambling because their families or their employers would not consider it respectable.

Midnight. The casino was full of the late-night crowd, visiting Americans, bands of Japanese corporation executives in identical suits, would-be sophisticates from the Swinging London scene, the inevitable Arabs and the equally inevitable sharks of both sexes. In the middle of all this superficial sophistication Terry Baker looked conspicuously average: blue blazer and flannels, hair shorter than was modish and in need of a wash, a shirt and tie suggesting better days. However, his general scruffiness was reassuring. No conman would have been happy with such an indifferent front.

I watched him carefully throughout his progression and found no fault with his paperwork or his behaviour. He never faltered in his calculations, always had time

in hand to select his plaques and chips for his next stake and showed no sign of yielding to a temptation particularly common among younger men, that of showing off. It is a dramatic experience of what one might call "theater" to find yourself the object of all attention at a roulette table. Some find it embarrassing, even terrifying, but just as many begin to show off in the limelight. Terry Baker sailed through the whole progression on red with neither blush nor bravado. Just after midnight he reached the table limit, calmly reverted to 1, 2, 3, 4, put on a 5-shilling stake and started to put his winnings in neat denominational piles.

As soon as I had seen the progression come to a successful conclusion I went to the club's washroom, a long and narrow room with basins spaced along one wall. As I was washing my hands and reflecting that things had gone remarkably smoothly, one of the casino bigwigs came into the room followed by four or five men whose dinner jackets served to accentuate their heavy physiques. I was at the basin farthest from the door. The looks on their faces told me not to expect a pat on the back for a jolly day's sport.

They stopped a few feet short of my basin, more or less penning me at the end of the washroom.

"Right, you little ponce—who d'you think you are?" said the stocky man whom I knew to be one of the club's senior officials and directors. Although we had been at pains not to look like an organized group it would not have taken any competent tableman long to realize that I was a link between the three people who had won so heavily that day, seeing me hovering at their sides, checking their notepads and occasionally murmuring advice.

Drying my hands and maintaining an outward calm, I decided there was no point in prevarication.

"I'm merely a club member with some friends who think they have a system to beat you. Have we broken any of the club rules?"

Whatever sangfroid I had acquired over the years seemed to be evaporating quickly before all those intensely unattractive faces.

"Don't give me any bloody fanny," snarled the director. I could see there was going to be no elegant way out of this situation. I was just trying to convince myself that things like this didn't happen in England, even in gaming clubs, when the door opened and a man came in, one of the regular patrons as far as I could tell.

"Just the bloke I want to see," he said to the casino director.

I shall never forget that man. He had on his head a dark brown wig, every artificial hair of it as conspicuous as a cloth cap on a blackbird. While the mob was looking at him I pushed past quickly and slammed the door behind me, safe again in the more crowded part of the casino.

Once the danger was over I had time to think and I realized that I had, in fact, had a very lucky escape. We had won over £5,000 ($14,000), in one day; most important from the casino's point of view we had won it systematically, which meant that we were potentially a major threat to its profits.

Realizing I had badly miscalculated the degree of tolerance the Regency's management would show to a winning group, I went back to the salon. A bit shaken, I had a quick whisky at the bar and only then returned to the tables. The first thing I noticed was that the team member who should have been handling black on the second table was missing.

"Where's Mr. Lee Kuan?" I asked Fredericks, a civil-servant member of the group, who was sitting next to

what had been Kuan's seat, now occupied by an aging Greek.

"Two of the staff asked if he would go to the club offices," said Fredericks, a rather dull man in his forties.

"Didn't you say anything?" I demanded. "I told everybody not to—oh forget it."

I went immediately to the reception desk and asked for someone in authority. The sleek young Frenchman at the desk, one of Mrs. Richardson's aptly named "greasy boys," said officiously, "What is the problem, monsieur?"

"I wish to know where my friend Mr. Kuan is," I said. "Two of your officials asked him to leave the salon."

He smirked and spread his hands expansively. "I know nothing of this, monsieur."

"In that case, I propose to search this establishment. If anyone tries to prevent me I shall call the police and inform them I have reason to believe Mr. Kuan has been kidnapped."

My brush with the management in the washroom had quickly made me aware of the fact that the Regency was not run by gentlemen. Hence my anxiety on Kuan's behalf. These people had obviously decided to pick on our weakest link.

I went up the stairs to the offices on the next floor. The first three rooms were empty. As I came to the door of the fourth I could hear voices. I did not hesitate.

Bursting into the room, I saw Kuan sitting in an armchair surrounded by the same men who had tried to corner me in the washroom. He was obviously being interrogated.

"What's the meaning of this?" I demanded.

"None of your business," said the director, a stocky and impressive man.

"This man is a friend of mine. You're taking advantage of his bad English. Why don't you grill me instead?"

"Don't you come barging in here throwing your bloody weight about," shouted one of the toughs.

"Release this man or you'll have thirty witnesses giving evidence against you on a kidnapping charge," was my counter. I nodded at Kuan to get up. One of the heavies made a move towards us, but the casino director waved him away.

They made no move to stop us as we left the office and went downstairs. It was late, and in view of what had happened I spread word round the two tables that we were ceasing operations for the day.

"Tell everybody I'm holding a meeting at my house —now," I said to Blake.

By half-past one that morning sixteen or seventeen of the group were sitting in my lounge. I asked Kuan to tell us what had happened to him. He said an official had asked him up to the office over some question about his membership. Then they had started asking him about the group—how many members did it have, who was behind it, what system were we using? When he had tried to leave they had pushed him back into the chair. That was when I appeared.

"I had a slight brush with them as well, in the toilets," I said. "It seems we've given them a bit of a shock, but I shouldn't imagine they'll try anything more serious."

Bateson, after a demonstration of sucking air through clenched teeth, complained petulantly: "We didn't bargain for intimidation. If I'd thought for a moment this would lead to trouble I wouldn't have considered the idea. My firm would react strongly if I got involved in anything disreputable—"

"Any scheme worth its salt must have some disadvantages," I said. "The greater the prize the bigger the obstacles. After all"—I started bringing money out of my

pockets, placing wads of tens and twenties on the table —"we haven't done too badly, have we? Mrs. Richardson won one thousand two hundred and seven pounds. Mrs. Heppenstall won two thousand and seventy-three pounds" —I put down another sheaf of notes—"and then Mr. Baker won two thousand and twenty. I make that five thousand three hundred. . . ." I stood back and let them gaze at the spread of notes on the table. Five thousand pounds ($14,000) in cash is not an everyday sight for many people. "Of course, divided among thirty-eight of us it isn't all that much," I went on. "But you won't have to pay tax on it."

They all stared at the money. Bateson had stopped his disapproving air-intake.

"Well," said Blake, looking round at the others, "I wouldn't like to think we could be frightened off *that* easily."

Heads nodded, though I noticed that Mr. Kuan's was not among them.

"What do you think we should do, Mr. Leigh?" asked Carter, the cement-yard manager.

"Carry on as we have started. We have the law on our side, not to mention moral right, so to hell with them!"

"Of course we'll go on," said Terry Baker, apparently speaking for everyone, including Bateson.

Then Blake got to his feet. It seemed he had never heard of an *informal* meeting.

"I regret to say that Mr. Sherlock broke one of your firmest rules today, Mr. Leigh. He spent most of his shift in the company of a young woman who picked him up at the table and sat beside him. They consumed a considerable amount of brandy, and there was a good deal of laughing and talking. It looked very bad."

He sat down. I had, in fact, noticed Sherlock chatting

to the woman but had assumed she was another player, the kind who wants to make jokes and is very difficult to ignore.

"*Did* she pick you up, Mr. Sherlock?" I asked. He was a clerk in his late twenties, unmarried, with mousy brown hair and a touch of acne.

"She did, I suppose," he said shamefacedly. "She just appeared at the next seat and started chatting. I got a bit carried away, I must admit."

Quite a few of us looked at him curiously, wondering what on earth any good-looking casino tart could have seen in him—he had not been winning, and his general manner, quite apart from his spots, was hardly that of a boudoir champion.

"You must realize the dangers in situations like that, Mr. Sherlock," I said. "You didn't know the woman. She could have been an informer planted by the management to find out what system we're using, or at best, a common tart out for your money. I cannot stress too highly the importance of not getting involved with other people while you are playing. This is work, not a spree. If we allow silly impulses to sidetrack us, we'll ruin the chances of profits altogether, not merely for ourselves but for the whole team."

Sherlock mumbled abjectly: "I can assure everyone it won't happen again."

I thought it was unlikely, too, for several reasons, so I let the matter rest.

Terry Baker put up his hand, the prevailing atmosphere possibly reminding him of school.

"I never really thought we'd win as much as that," he said. "Only—if we're stopping our progressions at the two-hundred limit, we're throwing money away, aren't we? I mean, I was having a real lucky streak, I could have gone on winning all night."

"Betting at the flat two hundred?" I said. "Surely you know that isn't how the system works. You won two thousand. If you'd gone on betting at two hundred a time without being able to progress upward you'd merely have been in the position of a man with two thousand pounds' capital coming to the table and risking large amounts on even-chance bets, a sure way to lose the lot."

"Aren't there any casinos without a limit?" he asked, unabashed.

"Yes, the Salle Privée, Monte Carlo. The minimum stake there is in the region of one pound. The Regency minimum is two shillings, although we are betting in shilling units. A losing sequence at the Salle Privée would mean an initial capital outlay of twenty times our present risk. It's an interesting thought, Mr. Baker, but I think we should forget it—at least until the group has accumulated a working capital of around a hundred thousand pounds."

"Oh." Baker sat back, looking sheepish.

"I've something else to say to you all," I continued. "I would like Mr. Blake to act as treasurer for the group. I have enough to do making sure the shifts are organized and watching you all at the table. There's the cashing up to do and then the division of our winnings. Would you do it, Mr. Blake—if everyone is agreeable?"

I daresay that if I had asked anyone other than Blake Bateson would have exploded. He was, after all, an accountant of some kind. His snobbery, however, made it possible for him to accept the superiority of an old Etonian.

"I should be happy to serve the group as treasurer," said Blake.

By the time I went with him to the front door and watched his bulky silhouette going down the drive to his car, dawn was breaking, and I had made him my "Num-

ber Two"—my second-in-command. For his trouble, he would receive 10 percent of our profits. He was one of the very few men whom I would have trusted at such short acquaintance to walk off into the night with five thousand pounds. My trust, however, owed less to any snobbery about his Eton tie than to the severely practical consideration that he had too much to lose to risk public scandal over £5,000. Family honour, and all that, in his case, wasn't a joke.

8

By 2 o'clock the next day—or rather, that afternoon—
eleven of the first shift and myself were in the coffee-
house near the Regency. The missing player was Peter
Vincent—as Blake had labelled him, our playboy friend.
I presumed he had lost interest, until, a few minutes later,
he walked into the coffee shop with the exaggerated control of a man who knows he has had too much. He was
trying hard to hide it. Only a stiffness of the tongue and
the delayed reactions of his eyes indicated that he was
loaded to the gills. As he sat down beside Mr. Milton, the
pubkeeper from Essex, he waved at one of the waitresses.

Blake gave me a nudge. Vincent asked the girl for a
black coffee and beamed at us all.

"Nice weather, isn't it?" he said. "Makes you feel
more like a gambol than a gamble. Eh?" He gave Milton
a dig in the ribs. "Don't laugh then."

"Are you fit?" I asked him.

"Yes," he answered, his eyes holding mine just long
enough to let me know he was in control.

"Woe betide you if you aren't," I said. Some of the
others looked curious, but no more was said. Vincent
stirred four lumps into his black coffee and drank it like
medicine, with a shudder.

As we came out onto the pavement Blake murmured angrily, "The bloody man is plastered!"

"All we are interested in is whether he can play roulette or not," I said. "Let's see how he behaves at the table."

Hostilities were declared within ten minutes of the first spin.

I was standing behind Blake when he signalled to one of the waiters and asked for a black coffee. The man turned his head away. Blake tried again, but there was no mistaking the cold shoulder. I caught up with the man.

"Will you kindly bring a cup of black coffee for that gentleman?"

He muttered something in French or Italian and walked off. Trivial as this may appear to the nonroulette player, it was more than just a pinprick. To the serious player, sitting at the table for hours at a stretch, the atmosphere heavy with smoke, a dry throat is serious enough a discomfort to upset his concentration. You'll hear people say that casinos offer wonderful food and drink at extremely low prices because their gambling profits enable them to be generous. In Las Vegas they do it with star-studded entertainment at nominal cost. It may be generosity—you will certainly pay well for it.

The waiter took twenty minutes to return with a jug of coffee on a tray.

As he edged close to Blake's shoulder he allowed the tray to tilt.

Hot black coffee poured down into the lap of Mrs. Richardson's black dress. I froze. A scene was inevitable.

Incredibly, Mrs. Richardson simply rubbed at her skirt with a handkerchief and went on with her calcula-

tions. I took the fellow to one side. He seemed cowed, her stoicism being the last reaction he could have expected.

"Now you will have to bring more coffee for that gentleman," I said firmly. This time it took forty minutes. However, he poured it without spilling a drop. (Later Blake said, "Of course he was cowed. English phlegm—it generally rattles the lesser breeds." I am *almost* sure he was joking.)

Around 4:30 P.M. Vincent had the start of a progression on *manque,* or low (the even-chance bet that the ball will fall in any number between one and eighteen). After twenty minutes it petered out, four successive losses wiping out his line of figures. He had only reached a stake of £2 or £3, but even if he had been up to £180 and the wheel had turned against him to the extent that all his figures had to be deleted, he would have lost all his winnings and his original capital, for that sequence, of 10 shillings. To win anything under the Reverse Labouchère you have to reach the limit on your progression or break the table. Every time you cross out your line you know you have lost ten units. (Think of the 1, 2, 3, 4 line. Your first bet is 1 + 4—5. Your second bet, if that one loses, is 2+3—5. If your second loses, you cross out your line. At any given moment the uncrossed figures in your line add up to what you are winning, and no matter how long the line or how high the individual figures if you lose often enough to delete all the figures, you lose all accumulated winnings—plus your original 10 units.)

Half an hour later Vincent ran into another progression. Drunk as he had been at 2:30 P.M. he now seemed fully in control of himself. From the first stake of 5 shillings his stakes steadily increased to £80 and

then £100 and then £150 ($420). As always happens in a casino the winning run quickly drew a crowd. This was why I had instructed the team to remain as inconspicuous as possible in dress and behaviour, for any degree of notoriety in a casino attracts so much attention one is surrounded by gaggles of curious spectators, many anxious to speak to you. People who are well mannered in normal life think nothing of butting in to ask questions about your system. You also become a magnet for every shark and parasite in the salon.

As we watched Vincent scribbling away at his figures I heard one elderly woman say she had come from Crockfords, the doyen of London's casinos, "to enjoy the fun." The news of a winning syndicate is never slow to spread in gaming circles. From a practical point of view publicity is the last thing one wants, but for a few moments I allowed myself to relax and enjoy the sight of Vincent applying all my lessons with apparently effortless precision, drunk as he had been a couple of hours before.

Sheer repetition finally brings an almost lyrical quality to the inevitable ritual of the roulette table, the tourneur giving the brass spokes of the wheel a twist, at the same time throwing the ball in the opposite direction, the skill of a French-trained operative ensuring that the little white ball completes exactly five circles of the wheel before it drops into a slot, the moment of silence as all eyes follow the numbers as the wheel slows, the swift precision of the croupier's stickwork as he drags in the losing stakes and shoves out the winning plaques and chips. There is the wheel and there is the ivory ball running round the track and here are we, putting ourselves for this brief moment at the mercy of the wheel's arbitrary whim.

Have we won? Yes! The gods have favoured us. It is

not mere money we have won, the money is only a token; no, we have been *recognized*.

Have we lost? We are sick in the stomach, we are fools and failures—but only for a moment. Next time the omens will be favourable, next time we will triumph, next time . . .

Vincent reached the table limit in under an hour. By then he was the star of the salon. All eyes were on him, the man who had mastered the unknowable. As he crossed out his line, wrote 1, 2, 3, 4 and placed a stake of 5 shillings the silence was such I could hear the faint roar of traffic from the street outside. As he started to arrange the pile of chips and plaques in neat piles he was watched by scores of people, some nakedly jealous, some childishly elated, a good many merely astonished.

Scarcely had Vincent started betting again at minimum stakes when Blake began a progression on red. By this time everybody in the salon seemed to be round that table, including the director and his muscular flunkeys. I wondered how easy it would be to succeed as a criminal if, like these fellows, one had an obviously criminal face.

Blake went on to reach the table limit. He had won £1,650 ($4,600). Vincent had won £2,150 ($6,000). The club's management was clearly on edge. When Mrs. Richardson asked a waiter for coffee I saw the director speak to him. He came back to Mrs. Richardson and said, "We are taking no more orders for coffee."

"Why not?" she said coolly. "It's half-past six in the evening, not the morning—what is it those other people are drinking?"

The waiter shrugged and smirked. All refreshment was shut off as far as we were concerned. When Blake's throat was so dry he couldn't go on without something

to drink my wife slipped into his chair to relieve him for a few minutes.

Immediately a young woman came round the table.

"Why did you take that chair?" she demanded shrilly. As nothing like this had happened before my wife was nonplussed.

"I beg your pardon," was all she could say. I went to her assistance.

"Has my wife done something wrong in taking this seat?" I asked the young woman, maintaining total formality in the event of her being an *agent provocateuse* under instructions to create the kind of incident that would justify them barring us.

"Yes, she has," she replied. "I've been waiting much longer than she has."

This was true. Pauline had been wandering about the club, having the occasional soft drink or a rest. According to the etiquette of the table a vacant chair goes to the person who has been standing longest.

"The gentleman whose chair this is has only gone to the bar for a quick drink," I said. "He will be back in a few seconds."

"I don't believe you," snapped the young woman.

"It's immaterial whether you believe me or not," I replied, controlling my temper. She was carrying a handful of plaques and may very well have been an ordinary member of the club—in which case her genuine anger would have suited the management even better. They could have simply chucked us out, but to bar people simply for winning too much would hardly have been good for business.

"My wife is giving up that seat to nobody but Mr. Blake," I said to the young woman. She pushed forward aggressively, obviously bent on forcing herself into the

seat when Pauline rose to let Blake back in. I saw him coming from the bar and quickly intercepted him.

"That young woman in the red silk dress standing behind Pauline, she's going to grab the chair," I explained. "We don't want to be involved in any scuffling, so let Pauline sit out the rest of your shift."

"Of all the damned cheek! Are you sure Mrs. Leigh will be able to cope?"

"I'm sure of it."

"That is a relief. By the way, what are we going to do about Vincent?"

"Congratulate him on handling his progression so well, I suppose."

"But he turned up drunk. We shouldn't let that pass without comment."

"If he makes a habit of it, we'll ditch him. But in a way, if it was just a lapse, I'm even more impressed."

"I don't follow that."

"A man who has a weakness and can superimpose his will on that weakness when the moment demands is a better bet for us than somebody who's never known temptation—they're the kind who go to pieces at the wrong time."

"It's your decision," he said.

"Yes, it is."

The rest of that day was without incident, though from the faces of the staff as we left it was clear that trouble was inevitable. While Blake went to drop our winnings into the bank's night safe a dozen or so of us headed for Twickenham. In the car Terry Baker asked me how many times we could expect to break the table or reach the limit in one week.

"Six people covering all the even chances through a whole day at one table could expect one progression per

day—with twelve of us covering two tables it would be two progressions a day. On average, of course."

"But the law of probability comes into it, doesn't it? Isn't it possible we could pull it off four or five times in one day?"

"We could also go four or five days on the trot without winning anything," said the gloomy Mr. Fredericks.

"You're both right," I said. "However, I'd rather have the occasional spell of a few days without a win than do it five times in a day. The losses would be catastrophic for the casino—we don't want to kill the golden goose."

"Yes, but we would have won a big bundle, a really big bundle," said Baker.

"I see that Mr. Kuan has not made an appearance today," I remarked, "and as he didn't ring me I assume he's been frightened off. Mr. Rogers has also bowed out. That leaves only thirty-five players, plus myself. This doesn't matter too much at the moment because the whole point of playing at the Regency is to give all of you a chance to accustom yourselves to real conditions and, ideally, for each of you to have coped with a progression. When we go to France, however, we will need thirty-six people to work the system profitably. It's possible I may be able to interest some of the people who came here originally."

"Does it matter if we're one or two short?" asked Simpson. "Surely that means more money for the rest of us?"

"It doesn't, in fact," I said. "The whole point is to cover the six even chances through every spin of the day. We've decided three shifts of four hours each are required to obviate undue physical strain. That means eighteen people per table. With thirty-six we can cover two tables. Suppose, however, we had only five people

for one of the tables. We would have to leave one of the even bets uncovered—that might be the one which would have thrown up a progression. Therefore those five are working a lot less profitably than the six at the other table. They would still, however, come in for an equal share of the day's profits. Do you see now why we have to work in multiples of six?"

It's doubtful if they did, but at that stage I was not really worried. Better to have too many than two few—and if I wasn't going to have a team of thirty-six I could pick and choose among the remainder to select the best team of eighteen. We had been playing for only four days. It was on the cards a few more would drop out when the going became tougher.

"I'd like to know what the hell we're supposed to do if we have another scuffle over seats like today?" Mrs. Richardson asked.

"Frankly I'm at a loss to give you any firm guidance," I said. "Somebody who's been standing for a long time expects to get the first vacant seat. It's the unwritten law of any decent casino. However, we are not there for amusement—one might say we are there to make our living. Having a seat is very important to us. On the other hand the management would dearly love some incident to give them an excuse to bar us. I'm afraid you'll have to play it by ear."

"Isn't it about time we set a date for going to France?" Baker asked impatiently.

"It's a little early for that," I said, beginning to wonder if Baker's impatience might be due to something more than youthful enthusiasm. "Only five or six of you have experienced a progression so far—until most of you have gone through the ordeal it would be unwise to transport the whole group to a strange casino a thousand miles away in

a foreign country. We're making our mistakes on our own doorstep, so to speak. I think we'll give it another three or four weeks."

Baker grimaced, but nobody else seemed inclined to support him.

As they were leaving it was almost dawn, and I was exhausted to the point of physical pain—yet *again* Baker bore down on me, waiting until the others were opening their cars before coming back up the drive.

"Could we have a quick word, just you and me?" he said.

We went back into the lounge, where the ashtrays were overflowing and the air was stale with smoke.

"Look, Norman," he began, "you know I said I was a salesman?"

"Yes?"

"Well, I'm not."

"Oh?"

"I'm a copper. Temporary detective constable, actually, south London."

"Not *again*, for God's sake," I groaned, staring out through the French windows at the first pink traces of sunrise.

9

"What do you mean—*not again*?" Terry Baker asked.

"I must be slipping—they infiltrated a detective inspector last time. You were planted to catch me in the act of conning these people, I take it."

"Yeah. Only—"

"Well, now you know it isn't a confidence trick, so good-bye. By the way, next time you play undercover man don't send three identically worded character references. I don't suppose there's any point in asking you to put in writing that I've been cleared of suspicion."

"What I was going to say is that I'm thinking of chucking my job in—you know, resigning."

"Why?"

"For the money, of course—when I put in my report that your scheme is kosher they'll take me off it, won't they?"

I was standing at the French windows, looking out at the garden and noticing how the early dawn light has a way of draining the colour from everything, as if one were watching black and white television. Tiredness was making me feel utterly detched. When I turned to look at him he was only a few feet away. His face was pale and tense with a stubble shadow that made him look almost dangerous.

"Are you telling me you want to resign from the police to join this scheme?"

"That's what I need to speak to you about—am I definitely going to be one of the lot you take to France?"

"What—you want to chuck in your job to play roulette for a living? Are you mad?" I laughed at him. He stared back. "You haven't even had any money yet," I said. "How do you know it *isn't* a bloody con trick? Blake and I might be in it together, we might—"

"No, I've checked him. He isn't going to risk his reputation and all that crap for a few grand."

"But you're going to risk your career and pension? When we divide that money it isn't going to add up to more than a couple of hundred each. You're mad. Go home and sleep on it and—"

"A couple of hundred for three or four days' work? You know the kind of money a detective constable makes? I got a wife and a baby and half the bloody time I can't afford a pint or a pack of fags."

"How many times have I told you I guarantee nothing? We could lose everything, the team could fall apart—I've run syndicates that didn't last a week, I've even had to go begging to the British consul for the fare home—you think you've found the key to the Bank of England?"

"You know what I think?" he said firmly. "I think we'll make a mint!"

"Perhaps we will. On the other hand we might be turned away from the Regency tomorrow, we might—"

"All I want to know is can you tell me if I'll be going to France?"

"Everything going to plan, I see no reason why you shouldn't. But that's not the point. What have you got ahead of you—twenty years at steady wages and then a healthy pension?"

He grimaced. "There are complications. I'm in a bit

of a dodgy situation financially. I do need to get some money somewhere—"

"Just remember—I advised you strongly against giving up your job. If you want to do it, then that's your business, of course. Personally I don't give a damn how stupid you are."

The first shift moved into the club at 2:55 P.M. the next day. They could not get the waiters to take their orders for coffee or soft drinks. I went to the bar and ordered three gin and tonics. As I picked up the glasses the bar manager said only waiters were permitted to carry drinks out of the bar.

"Why won't the waiters serve us then?" I demanded. He merely grinned. Saying nothing, I drank the three gins one after the other and walked back to the salon.

The first shift played to 6:45 P.M. without encountering a progression, and I was checking that the second shift had all turned up when Mrs. Heppenstall hit a progression on *pair* (even). At 7 P.M. the second shift managed to take over without any arguments about seating. Mrs. Heppenstall remained at her place to see the progression to a conclusion. When her stakes reached £40 ($112) she looked up at me and said, with a distinct roguishness: "Would you believe it, Mr. Leigh, I've got another of those mushrooms?"

It was an entirely appropriate description for progressions, appearing suddenly and unexpectedly and then billowing out in an upwards explosion of wins.

"I think Mrs. Heppenstall has just added a new term to the language of gaming," I said to Blake. He raised his eyebrows and indicated that I should look behind me. The club's director was standing at the other side of the table with a group of his less Neanderthal employees, those who could read and write presumably—they started

to record Mrs. Heppenstall's staking pattern in notebooks. As her stakes went on rising the inevitable crowd flocked to the table. The club director looked ready to suffer a stroke, his fleshy face becoming diffused with blood. It was one of those eerie moments when one has the curious feeling that it is not real life one is participating in but a stage play. Craziness seemed to be in the air. Anything could happen, and when it did it was a large foreign woman, possibly Dutch, who elbowed her way vigorously to the table. She was in her sixties, rather grandly dressed. She rummaged into a large square handbag and produced a handful of high-denomination plaques and an ear trumpet.

Yes, an ear trumpet. London was then supposed to be the "Swinging" capital of the world but youth and beauty don't rate so highly in a casino as cash, a commodity that is usually and regrettably in the hands of the old and ugly. Muttering to herself in guttural undertones, this silver-haired matron finally turned to me: "Can you tell me what is last number that comes up?"

"Seven," I said.

Cocking an imperial head to one side, she put the ear trumpet in place. "What you say, please?"

"Seven," I said into the trumpet.

She shook her head.

"Seven," I said again in a louder voice.

She frowned. Taking out my notepad, I wrote a large 7 on a blank page. She peered at it and shook her head again.

"Can you make it more large please—I cannot see well."

I wrote a 7 that was at least six inches high. She screwed up her eyes, failed to comprehend—and dived once more into the big handbag to produce a *magnifying glass*.

"Ah—*seven*," she exclaimed. Nodding wisely, she leaned

past Mrs. Heppenstall and put a £5 plaque on seven. It is quite a common hunch among gamblers to back the same number to come up twice running. However, in the time taken to give her the information there had been another spin, twenty-eight having come up. She lost—£5, no doubt just a blur before her eyes.

This incident, not untypical of the underlying madness in a casino, may explain the hostility shown towards us by the management. We knew what we were doing, and for that reason we were a genuine threat. That half-deaf, myopic but wealthy Dutchwoman might occasionally win at odds of 35 to 1, giving her £175 if by any chance her vision allowed her to get the bet on a number, but her regular losses would more than make up for it. Most casino patrons are mentally comparable to the dull-faced queues one sees waiting in draughty streets for bingo halls to open—the stakes are higher and the clothes are better, but basically they share the same lack of scientific knowledge and for the thrill of an occasional win are happy to go through a childish rigmarole time and time again.

When Mrs. Heppenstall's progression reached the stage where her next bet would have been £222 she calmly scored out all her figures, wrote 1, 2, 3, 4 on a clean page and put down a 5-shilling chip. She had won 40,000 units— an even £2,000 ($5,600). This was just too much for the management of the Regency. After a short confab with the director, the Chef de Partie, who supervises play at the tables, announced in a loud voice that *all* roulette tables were being closed for the rest of the day, although the other games, *trente et quarante*, blackjack and so on, were continuing as usual.

"We're beginning to hurt them," said Blake as we cashed Mrs. Heppenstall's chips and plaques. He went off to pay the £2,000 into the night safe while the rest of us went back to Twickenham. Inside, I took the floor, fore-

stalling any inclination the group might have to talk itself into a panic.

"Ladies and gentlemen," I said, "they closed down the roulette tables because they didn't want us to win any more money. We are not mindreaders, so it is idle to speculate what they will do next. The only way to find out is to be at the Regency at three o'clock tomorrow afternoon, take up our usual positions and wait and see. It should be interesting."

"They'll ban us, won't they?" said Milton, the pubkeeper from Essex.

"They could have done that today," I said. "I have the feeling they'll try something else."

"Suppose we are banned, what will we do then?" asked Fredericks. "You said a month's training in real conditions was essential."

"I consider that it would be suicidal to begin operations in France until every one of us is absolutely *au fait* with the method and with every contingency that can arise at a roulette table. If we were to be barred, I think we should all have to buy a small wheel and practice with something like five hundred spins a day."

The Regency's management made its move before the first spin of the wheel the following afternoon. Our first shift was preparing to place the opening stakes of 5 shillings when the Chef de Partie made an announcement.

"Ladies and gentlemen, the casino directors wish to inform you of a change in the club rules. Henceforth the minimum bet for the roulette tables will be ten shillings, not two shillings as before. Thank you."

Blake looked at me.

"We'll pack it in for today," I said. "I'll stay here and wait for the second and third shifts and warn them not to come."

"Want me to stay with you?" Blake asked.

"No point in both of us wasting a day. No, I'll see you at seven tomorrow."

The following evening most of the group was at my home, looking depressed. Knowing that my chance of taking a properly trained group to France was in the balance, I used a bit of practical psychology.

"Ladies and gentlemen," I began, "as you all know, the Regency has raised the minimum bet from two shillings to ten shillings [$1.40] and I have no doubt this was solely to throw us out of gear. Our staking method requires bets of five, six, seven, eight and nine shillings at the outset of a progression. These are now ruled out. Before I give you the simple answer to this maneuver I'll ask Mr. Blake to give his report."

Blake had a briefcase (new, black, brass fitments) and a cash book (new, black, gilt lettering embossed on the cover). Sounding like the church garden-fete treasurer, he intoned his report.

"On day one," he began, "we had no winnings. Day two we had no winnings. On day three we won five thousand three hundred pounds from three progressions. On day four we won three thousand eight hundred pounds from two progressions. On day five we won two thousand pounds from one progression. Our total winnings so far are, therefore, eleven thousand one hundred pounds [$31,000]. I have a printout of the bank statement to verify these figures."

He looked round, but nobody was inclined to challenge his accuracy. Maurice Nathan leaned forward to congratulate Mrs. Heppenstall on being the only one who had experienced two progressions. She blushed girlishly.

"The money is allocated as follows," Blake went on. "Under the agreed arrangements Mr. Leigh and I each

take ten percent. By the way, there are odd shillings to all these amounts, but I am leaving these in the bank to keep the account open, if no one has any objection. Twenty percent comes to two thousand two hundred and twenty pounds between Mr. Leigh and myself. That leaves eight thousand eight hundred and eighty pounds. As Mr. Rogers and Mr. Kuan have dropped out, and as I do not propose to pay myself twice—"

"Hear, hear," said a deep male voice.

"—that means thirty-four equal shares, two hundred and sixty-one pounds each [$730], with a balance of a few pounds which I also propose to leave in the bank. I have here an envelope for each of you. . . ."

Reading out names from the list in his cash book, he began handing out the envelopes. I waited until they were counting bank notes.

"It's not exactly a fortune," I began.

"How do I put it down on my tax form?" Keith Robinson asked innocently.

"You don't breathe a word of this to the Inland Revenue, you fool," Bateson snapped.

"I think Mr. Robinson was joking," I said.

"Course I was," Robinson exclaimed, pretending to be aggrieved. "I've never seen a tax form in my life, have I?"

"It's not a fortune, but it's encouraging considering that we are supposed merely to be learning the method," I went on. "Now, as to what happens next—my solution to their increase in the table minimum is merely to maintain your paperwork up to ten shillings without physically staking any money. Once your calculations take you over ten shillings you can start putting down stakes. Similarly, when a progression comes down below ten shillings you will revert to paperwork alone. On average the results will

be the same as if the limit had not been altered. In fact there will be a slight percentage advantage to us in that zero will be taking nothing from us while we're working below ten shillings. Is that clear to everybody?"

"It seems absurdly simple," said Blake.

"Perhaps," I said, drily. "It won't make the management any happier to have a lot of people occupying seats when they are betting merely on paper. They will probably try to provoke scenes, so from now on be doubly careful."

Day Seven. Our first shift gave the croupiers at both tables something to think about. Twelve people seated at the tables and doing involved paperwork without placing any chips on the green baize? The casino boss was summoned in short order. I watched his plump face carefully as he went into a muttered discussion with the Chef de Partie.

Before they could come to any decision Mr. Hopplewell ran into a progression which lasted for fifty minutes. Everybody watched with fascination—disgust in the case of the director—as shilling stakes turned into pounds, then tens of pounds and scores of pounds. And then hundreds.

A curious change came over Hopplewell. Aged sixty, florid, overweight, gruff and withdrawn, the man who had professed contempt for all forms of gambling, he began to change with each winning bet. Bravado is the only word for it. Each new pile of plaques and chips went down with a flamboyant flourish. He grinned at various women hanging round the table, smacked his hands noisily after each win, even threw a £5 plaque to the croupier as a tip.

Then I drew in my breath. I could see the four-digit figures on his notepad, and before he had added the two at either end of the line I knew his next stake would be £225 ($630).

Instead, however, of crossing out his figures and revert-

ing to 1, 2, 3, 4 he began to assemble a handful of plaques, apparently ready to place a bet above the table maximum.

Remembering that he had fluffed our first chance of a winning progression, even I, witness to every form of casino madness, was surprised at how quickly he had succumbed to a temptation which besets many roulette players, the latent desire to achieve notoriety as an arrogant devil who rides roughshod over petty rules and regulations. Taking money is only the most obvious way the table has of destroying people, perhaps even the *least* dangerous.

Hopplewell—unimaginative, surly, hostile, probably bored by life but frightened at how quickly it was passing—had made himself wealthy by stolid application to commerce. Suddenly he had become a daredevil, a pirate, a dashing hero, liberated by a brass wheel, a little ivory ball and a few plastic discs. Other men envied him. Attractive women admired him. In a few moments he had rediscovered the sweet bravado of youth.

At the time I was too angry to indulge in such fanciful philosophizing. I got to his elbow just as he was assembling a handful of plaques. He looked round to make sure he had the attention of all the people jammed at the table. Then he caught my eye.

He gave me a slow wink and put the plaques back on the green baize in front of him. Smiling slyly, he scored out his line of figures and wrote 1, 2, 3, 4. Excited faces waited to see what he would do next. He scribbled the figure 5 on his pad and then sat back, arms crossed, lips tightening in a little smile of triumph. His face was wet with perspiration. The club's director went into agitated conversation with his associates, all of them keeping us under hostile surveillance. Blake came back from the restaurant.

"Hopplewell has just won two thousand or there-

abouts," I said. "You know what he did? He made as though he was going to put down a stake far above the limit! He was only joking, but—"

"They were talking about it in the restaurant. I hurried through my meal so that I wouldn't miss it. Those chaps don't look too happy now, do they? By the way, what would they have done if he'd tried to stake over the limit?"

"The croupier would have spotted it before the ball was thrown, and he'd have been told quietly to remove his bet. At least that's what normally happens—I don't know what this lot would have done."

"I imagine they're making feverish plans to deal with us now."

At about five o'clock Mrs. Richardson hit a progression on black. As soon as her stakes began to rise the director and two or three of his henchmen crowded round her chair.

They began to talk at her from all sides.

"Would you like a cigarette, madam?" said one, shoving a packet in front of her face. She shook her head and went on with her calculations.

"Can I get madam some coffee?" said another. She shook her head again. I eased in close behind her and leaned down.

"Say nothing to them. Ignore them completely," I murmured.

She nodded calmly and put on a stake of £50, her right eye slightly screwed up against smoke rising from the cigarette she was forced to keep between her lips while her hands were occupied.

It was an incredible spectacle, three or four aggressive men doing everything short of physical assault to distract a handsome young woman, who resolutely refused to be distracted. When she reached the table limit of £200 and

reverted to 1, 2, 3, 4 she had won just over £3,000. The faces of the director and his staff were a picture of vicious frustration.

"I think I'll have a bite in the restaurant," I said to Blake. "You keep an eye on things here."

"I daresay the worst they can do is chuck us out," he said.

"You wouldn't find that—embarrassing?"

He huffed at the very idea.

In the restaurant while I was waiting to be served, two waiters began to discuss our group. Perhaps they knew who I was.

"They've just won another whack," said one with noticeable relish, apparently unsympathetic to his employers' suffering.

"You wait. They won't be here much longer," said the other.

"How come?"

"You'll see," said the second one, tapping his nose.

I paid my bill and went back to the tables. We did not have another progression that night. None of the staff said a word to us when we left at 3 A.M. Keith Robinson and I went with Blake and deposited the cash in the bank.

The Regency management dropped their bombshell before the first spin of the wheel the following afternoon. Our first shift was seated at the two tables, lines of 1, 2, 3, 4 on clean pages of their notebooks, chips piled neatly on the table, when the Chef de Partie made an announcement.

"Ladies and gentlemen, the management wishes to initiate a change in the rules for roulette. The minimum stake on even chances will remain ten shillings—and henceforth only multiples of ten shillings [$1.40] will be accepted as stakes on the even chances. Thank you."

The others looked at me. To those nearest I said, "Cash your chips at the desk and we will go to my house for a meeting. Spread the word around, would you?"

"Why aren't we playing?" Terry Baker demanded, catching up with me as I made for the exit.

"They found the way to stop us, of course."

"What do you mean? All we got to do is bet in units of ten bob."

"Is that all? Are you prepared to lose a hundred pounds a day instead of ten?"

"I don't see—"

"I'll explain it later at my place."

The entire management seemed to be present, most of them smirking, as our party reached the exit. Knowing there was no possibility of our playing there again, I went across to the director.

"I'm surprised it took you so long to find the answer," I said cheerfully.

He shrugged. "No hard feelings?" he said. "Only we couldn't have your lot hogging the seats and sitting there all day betting peanuts, could we?"

"Peanuts? Sixteen thousand pounds, give or take a hundred or two? I think we gave you a good run for your money."

"We don't mind our members winning a bit."

We both smiled. "As we shall not be returning I wonder if I could ask you to do me a favour," I said.

"What is it"

"Quite a number of my associates will be turning up throughout the rest of the day. Could your staff pass on the word that they should go straight to Norman Leigh's house? I would wait for them myself but I hate the atmosphere of casinos."

"Delighted," he said. "Come back soon, won't you—in about two hundred years!"

"We should go straight to the police," Blake protested when we were on the pavement. Our withdrawal had been witnessed by a lot of people, and he was mortified.

"They outmaneuvered us. It's as simple as that," I said. "They found a way to make the system ruinously expensive, and there's nothing we can do about it. Do you have yesterday's winnings with you?"

"Yes.

"What does it come to?"

"You and I split one thousand and forty-five pounds [$2,920], and the others share four thousand one hundred and eighty between them—about a hundred and twenty-three pounds each [$344]. Why?"

"It might be enough."

"Enough for what?"

"To make it a fair wind for France, of course."

By dint of phoning we managed to contact most of the other members of the group before they left work or home for the second and third shifts, and by eight o'clock that night they were all present in my lounge. Eventually even the least mathematically minded grasped what the Regency's management had achieved by making ten shillings the basic unit for betting on the even chances.

"Your line wouldn't be one, two, three, four," I explained. "It would be ten, twenty, thirty, forty. Our capital risk would be multiplied exactly ten times. Instead of each of you bringing ten or fifteen pounds a day you would have to bring a hundred or more."

"But the system would still work just the same," said Simpson. "In fact, we'd be winning a lot more, wouldn't we?"

"We're not all rich enough to invest a hundred a day, Mr. Simpson," I said. "The whole point of the Reverse Labouchère is that it enables us to deal in shillings while

we are losing, and that is most of the time. If your line is ten, twenty, thirty, forty, you would be losing fifty units each time you crossed it out—that's two pounds ten shillings. And when we *did* get a winning progression we wouldn't win any more. They haven't increased the maximum bet, have they?"

"So where do we go now?" asked Milton, the burly pub landlord.

"There are plenty of casinos in London," said Terry Baker. "Even if we only last a few days in each of them, we can still pick up thousands. Next time we can be a bit cleverer about disguising ourselves as a group."

"News travels with the speed of light in those circles," I said. "As soon as we appeared at another casino they would know who we were and what we were up to. They would simply change their staking requirements as the Regency did today. No, I think the time has come."

"To go to France?" said Fredericks, making it sound like a trip in the tumbril. "But you said we needed a full month's training in a real casino, and I haven't even been through a mushroom yet."

"We have no choice," I said. "All the London casinos now know how to drive us away. At least in France the staking limits are fixed by government regulation. Nothing short of legislation can alter them. It's France now or nothing."

Blake had suggested that we postpone a decision, but I had explained to him that to delay now would probably kill the whole thing. A few weeks before none of these people had ever played roulette seriously—many had never been inside a casino. I had led them gently into what they regarded as an adventure, and so far they had all done well enough out of it. Most of them had missed the various threatening ploys used by the Regency management to intimidate a few individuals. They still regarded the whole

thing as a novelty, but give them a few weeks of inactivity and they might begin to realize how deep these waters could be. The time to strike was now.

"We've had enough practice sessions, I think," I said. "They're boring and they take up a lot of time. I propose that we set a date for France. While Mr. Blake is handing out his envelopes will you all think seriously of how soon you can make arrangements to go? How does a fortnight from now sound?"

Blake stood up with his cash book. As he sonorously ploughed through the figures I watched faces. I needed eighteen people to give us three shifts of six covering one table twelve hours a day. Any more than eighteen would cost the group money. If all thirty-four decided to come I was going to be in an embarrassing situation.

Waiting until the white envelopes were being torn open, I said, "Well, ladies and gentlemen, I realize it's shorter notice than we anticipated, but how do you feel about leaving for the Riviera in two weeks?"

Not one hand went up!

I allowed myself no sign of disappointment.

"If you had a month to get ready, how many could make it then?"

Six hands went up.

"Suppose we set it for late September, that would give you seven weeks. How many could make it then?"

Five more hands went up.

For a moment I had an urge to scream at the rest of them. They had done all those weeks of practice, they could see the system was all I claimed for it, they had each made £400 ($1,120), from what was supposed to be only a dress rehearsal. What more did I have to do, damn it?

Bateson got to his feet.

"I don't see why we should rush into it," he said. "I could probably get a week or two off in the spring."

"Look, we're psychologically ready for it right *now*," I exclaimed.

"It's all very well for some people," he went on, glancing round the lounge ceiling, clearly intimating that I was one of the idle rich, "but those of us with families and jobs can't just be dashing off abroad when the mood takes us."

"Seven weeks' notice is hardly dashing off, Mr. Bateson," I said patiently. "You did know from the start that my intention was to take the group to France in the late autumn."

"Yes, but of course none of us had any idea then whether your scheme would work."

"Well? You've each won four hundred pounds already—"

"Could be we've pushed our luck as far as it'll go," he said quickly. I eyed him coldly.

"How does one win a lot of money except by pushing one's luck?"

Bateson sensed that he had strong support. There was a new note of amusement in his voice as he looked at me across the lounge. "I think you've got some romantic notion about France, Mr. Leigh," he said patronizingly. "The rest of us can't be expected to share your private dreams, can we?"

I swallowed hard. "Whatever my original reasons for wanting to take the group to France, the fact is that we've had it as far as any London casino is concerned. Therefore, to carry out the scheme France is now a practical necessity —unless you'd rather make it Las Vegas."

Bateson smiled. "I don't think I can be accused of being a stick in the mud. I wouldn't be here if I was. How-

ever, let's be sensible about this. We haven't done too badly, but we have no guarantee—"

"Guarantee?" I snapped. "Has the government seen fit to put roulette on the National Health Service? Until gambling becomes part of the welfare state I'm damned if—"

Sensing the ultimate horror—raised voices—Blake rose to his feet, wielding his sense of propriety like a bull-fighter's cape.

"This is Mr. Leigh's show," he said. "We all knew what he planned when we joined the group. If seven weeks is too soon for most of you, why don't those who can get away leave for France at the end of September? We can start playing immediately and the rest of you can join us as soon as it is convenient."

"Going to stay in the south of France for the winter, are you?" said Bateson.

"As long as we can milk casinos I'll stay in France for the rest of my life," said Keith Robinson.

"Me too," said another, glaring ferociously at Bateson.

Several said they would try hard to bring forward holiday entitlements and the like but I could see they were itching to get away. Some credit was due to them for having come this far, however, and I thanked each for the hard work he or she had put in, saying that if anyone changed his mind not to hesitate to call me up. They filed out.

I smiled at the ten who remained and were prepared to take the plunge. For a few moments I had been depressed and angry at what seemed like mass betrayal, but that soon passed. Counting Blake, I had eleven, not necessarily the best roulette players nor even the most attractive personalities—but the best for my purposes. They wanted to do it almost as badly as I did and to me that made them ideal.

As might have been expected, all those who had enjoyed the spicy thrill of a winning progression were ready to take the scheme to its next phase, but there were also a few surprises. The eleven left in my lounge that night were:

OLIVER BLAKE, thirty-two, single, stockbroker.

EMMA RICHARDSON, thirty-five, married, housewife (formerly a commercial designer).

LETTICE HEPPENSTALL, fifty-four, widow, housewife.

KEITH ROBINSON, twenty-six, single, "clerk."

TERRY BAKER, twenty-seven, married, one child, policeman.

ALEC SHERLOCK, twenty-nine, single, office manager.

MAURICE NATHAN, thirty-seven, single, textile industry executive.

SYDNEY HOPPLEWELL, sixty, divorced, company director.

GEORGE MILTON, forty-seven, married, pubkeeper.

THOMAS FREDERICKS, forty-one, single, civil servant.

PETER VINCENT, thirty, married (separated), company director.

"There's nothing to worry about," I said to Blake. "We've got the makings of a very good team here. We'll have to rethink the shift situation, that's all."

"But you told us eighteen was the absolute minimum."

Looking at Mrs. Richardson, I kept a straight face and said, "One couldn't expect a gaming coup to go as smoothly as a convocation of suffragan bishops, Mr. Blake. We'll all just have to work harder at it. But there will be fewer of us to share the profits."

"That little bastard Bateson spoiled everything," said Mrs. Richardson. "Perhaps if we could talk to the others without him—"

"No, the whole scheme depends on total enthusiasm," I said. "If they can be put off so easily at this stage, how could we rely on them if things turned rough, especially in a foreign country?"

"Advertise again?" Vincent suggested, with untypical practicality.

"Never! Six or seven weeks ago I started out by interviewing nine hundred and fifty-one people—and produced eleven of you!"

"We could do it in two shifts working six hours each," suggested Sherlock.

"Could you cope with that?" I asked, wondering why it was I had ever disliked the man. The self-indulgence of emotion was over. Those who had dropped out twenty minutes before might as well have been dead. Certainly they were already fading from *my* memory. As well as Sherlock, I had never really cared much for Vincent, Fredericks, Hopplewell and Milton, who was very much the old-soldier type, full of mother-in-law jokes and embarrassingly vocal about his allegedly monstrous wife. Yet now that they had selected themselves, they seemed like the salt of the earth.

"I'll tell you, I graft eighteen bloody hours a day in my pub and I don't get four hundred quid a week tax-free for it," Milton said, adding ruefully, "I don't even get any thanks for it. Six hours is nothing."

Blake pointed out that there were only eleven players. "Out of all those who've just left, isn't there *one* person we could persuade to join us?"

"No," I replied. "That's very bad psychology. We must go into this together on the same basis, not because I've talked you into it but because you are a hundred percent behind it. Anybody we persuaded to come against his better judgment would always have a good excuse for carping and grumbling. I suggest we give it a day or two before we allow depression to set in. Some of the others

might change their minds—as long as their decision is spontaneous."

I waited for several days. Occasionally I was tempted to phone Blake and say to hell with it, let's have a bash with what we've got, but if the years hadn't taught me wisdom exactly, they had provided enough painful lessons about going off half-cocked. We might be able to permutate eleven into two daily shifts of six, but the strain would be enormous and if only one of the team cracked up, the whole thing would collapse.

"This time it's got to go like clockwork, or I don't do it at all," I told Pauline a few days later, having heard nothing from any of those who had dropped out.

"That *would* be a pity after all the work you've put into it," she said loyally.

Then suddenly I had the answer: "Mrs. Harper-Biggs!"

"*Who?*"

"She was the one who cracked up and wanted us to hare off to the Belgian Congo—she'd be ideal for our twelfth player. I bet you she'd come."

"She doesn't sound very ideal if she cracked up."

"It was only because she had to work very long hours. I'll go down to Bournemouth and see her."

"That was a long time ago—she might have moved— she might even be dead."

"Her kind don't die. Anyway, I'm only risking a few gallons of petrol."

I rang Blake. "Look, I think I know the very person to make up the team," I said when he came on the phone. "Can you drive us down to Bournemouth tomorrow?"

"Tomorrow? That's a bit short notice, I don't really know if—"

"Good. It will be better with you there. Don't want her to think it's another of my one-man wild-goose chases. Pick me up about ten, eh? By the way, whatever you do— don't mention Italians."

10

The surly young maid who showed us into the lounge with the huge fireplace was a new girl, but nothing else seemed to have changed in the ten or eleven years since I had come to this house as a young clerk in a ten-pound suit. Certainly Mrs. Harper-Biggs had changed so little we might have parted only the day before.

"Mr. Leigh!" she exclaimed. "When the girl announced the name I couldn't believe it was you. I'm so glad to see you. I've so often wanted to tell you how sorry I was for letting you down."

I introduced Blake and we all shook hands. For a blessed moment I thought Blake was going to shake *my* hand, so extended were the social niceties. We sat down and exchanged the usual pleasantries. I was impatient to tell her the reason for our unexpected visit, but Blake seemed to have forgotten why we were there in his enthusiasm for complimenting her on her paintings and furnishings. Mrs. Harper-Biggs asked me if I would pull the bellrope. On this occasion it was not her small, dutiful husband who appeared but the aggressively silent maid. Mrs. Harper-Biggs asked her to bring a tray of coffee. Blake said a few admiring words about yet another of her paintings, to my eyes just a dark rectangle with the barely discernible outlines of a face with ferrety eyes.

"Family heirloom, I suppose," he said.

"No. Herbert bought it at a sale."

Coffee was served in exquisite china cups so small one sip was sufficient to require a refill. Before she got round to giving Blake a guided tour I decided to interrupt.

"Mrs. Harper-Biggs," I began, "I've come down with Mr. Blake from London to ask you a question. You remember the last time I came to see you in this room?"

"I do, indeed. By the way, poor Herbert passed away four years ago, dear man. More coffee, Mr. Blake?"

"Excellent," said Blake.

"And what is this question?" she asked me.

"I have formed a group to go to that same casino where we tried out the Fitzroy system all those years ago. We're leaving at the end of September. The method we're using is much simpler than the Fitzroy, and with twelve players we'll be able to work in shifts of only six hours. Would you like to join the group? I realize you may not have altogether happy memories of our last venture—"

"The number of times I could have kicked myself for being so silly," she said to Blake. "Mr. Leigh had a wonderful method for winning money, and I let him down badly. End of September, you said? I'd be delighted to come."

"Naturally I don't ask you to commit yourself without hearing more about it—"

"Mr. Leigh, I am a fifty-six-year-old widow, with no relatives and a few boring friends who probably find me even more boring than I find them. Nothing would give me greater pleasure than to go with you. Besides, going away for a spell will give me a good excuse to get rid of that awful girl. She drives me mad with her continual sniffing."

"Sniffing?" said Blake. "Can't she use a handkerchief?"

"No, *disapproval*. She comes from a background of

religious dementia. It's very common in rural Dorset. I think she suspects me of entertaining strange men late at night when she goes home. Mr. Blake, I haven't offered to show you my collection."

"You would have to come up to my place in Twickenham for a bit of practice in the system," I said.

"Wonderful. I can go to the Natural History Museum in Kensington. Do you know anything about beetles and such things, Mr. Blake?"

"Fascinating," he said.

The more I saw of the group during the next seven weeks the more confident I became. Here was no collection of dilettantes and drunken eccentrics but sober, reliable people from diverse walks of life united by an enthusiasm which owed more to common sense than fantasy. Terry Baker was the only one I had doubts about—simply because his enthusiasm ran away with him. At one meeting in the middle of September he told me he had resigned from the police.

"Well, on your head be it," I said. "I would have thought that with a wife and young child you would have been better advised to stick to a good career with prospects and a pension. But you're a grown man, and I'm not your guardian."

He smiled. "You're too bloody cautious, Norman. Look, I want to show you something."

He brought out a notebook and showed me page after page of figures. "I've been putting in the hours on my toy wheel at home," he said. "That's a real progression, just the way the wheel threw it up. I was working without a table limit. Know what the winnings are? Only four hundred thousand pounds, that's all."

I checked his figures and could find no flaw with them

—except, of course, that they were only on paper. Baker showed them to the others later. Milton was ecstatic. "One of them and we'd be set for life! No more crates of bloody ale to hump up and down. First thing I'd book myself on a world cruise and throw away the return ticket!"

"Yes, but it depends on playing without a table limit," I said.

"The Sally Privy!" exclaimed Baker, who had remembered the name of the Monte Carlo establishment I had once talked about where no table limit operates.

"The Salle Privée indeed! For a start we'd need capital of a thousand each. Our lines would be composed of six-digit figures—all very feasible in the comfort of your own home, but could you maintain an astronomical line like that in a crowded casino?"

"We could buy larger notepads," drawled Vincent.

"Or hire a portable computer," said Mrs. Richardson.

Baker said he still thought we should try it. The Regency management had taken only eight days to beat us; in France they might be quicker, he reasoned. Why not go for the big one straight off? To end this discussion without giving him cause for resentment I said that if we did extraordinarily well in the Casino Municipale I, for one, might be willing to use my winnings to have a crack at the Salle Privée in Monte Carlo. Baker seemed satisfied with that.

"How long do you expect us to be staying down there on the Riviera?" asked Sherlock.

"If the shekels are rolling in I won't be breaking a leg to dash back to the arms of my old woman, believe me," said Milton.

"You can count on me to stay as long as we're showing a profit," said Maurice Nathan. "My last firm went kaput,

and the doctor says my nerves are bad. A change of scenery and a chance to make myself some capital, just what I need."

Blake said his father was willing to give him indefinite leave of absence from the family firm. Keith Robinson said he was between jobs anyway. One by one each person indicated that he would postpone any commitments. That left only Fredericks.

"Bit tricky I'd imagine, switching holidays about in the Civil Service," I said to that somber gentleman.

He fidgeted and looked at his large, pale hands. "No, I'm all right," he said. Then he looked at me sheepishly and said, "I handed in my resignation on Friday."

"You didn't, did you?"

"Yes, I'd used up all my holiday entitlement. My mother was ill in May, and I had to look after her."

I asked him to stay behind when the others left. For the headstrong Baker to chuck in his job was one thing; he had hinted that he was already in some kind of trouble and in any case he didn't strike me as the type who would have lasted thirty years at any job let alone the police. But Fredericks was forty-one and extremely passive, and I did not want him ruining his life—to be honest, I did not want to run any risk of being blamed, however inaccurately, for feeding him false illusions.

"It's not too late to withdraw your resignation, is it?" I asked, pouring him a stiff whisky.

"Look, Norman—you don't mind me calling you Norman, do you?"

"Not in the slightest."

"It's just that Mr. Blake always—"

"Blake has been to Eton; we have to make allowances."

"I said my mother was ill in May—actually she'd been ill for twenty years. I had to look after her. She's dead now—"

"I'm sorry to hear that."

"Oh, don't be sorry. She was a selfish old woman and she stopped me from having much of a life. When I saw your advertisement in the *Telegraph*—this will sound stupid, but I don't have many friends really and being with all of you and coming to this house—well, it's almost like having a family, do you know what I mean? I don't think I've ever enjoyed anything so much in my whole life. When you wanted to fix a date for going to France I knew I'd have to bow out because I'd already used up my holidays for this year. Then I just thought—why should I give up the only interesting thing that's happened to me for years? I'm not chucking away a fancy career by any means. I'm only a low-grade clerk really. You keep warning us not to expect too much—I don't care if we don't make a penny. It will be the most exciting experience of my whole life. My mother—well, tell you the truth I've never even had a girlfriend, not seriously." He looked at his watch, painfully embarrassed by this confession. I brought over the bottle of Scotch.

"It's getting late," he said apologetically. "The last tube goes from Richmond in twenty minutes, I—"

"For a man who's chucked in a safe governmental career to go gambling on the Riviera it's a bit late to be worrying about the last bloody tube train, Thomas," I said. "Have another whisky and let's finish this bottle."

The following week we set out for France. The three younger men, Robinson, Baker and Sherlock, went by plane; the others by car; I by train, alone.

At 8:30 on the morning of Tuesday, September 27, I kissed Pauline good-bye on the steps in front of our rented house, without which the Mushroom Mob (as Robinson had called us) could not have been.

"Give me a ring when you get there. I should be down

by the end of the week," Pauline said. "And take care of yourself."

"Are you really sure you want to come?"

"Of course. I want to make sure you're managing without me. Good-bye, darling. Take care of yourself."

On the night train south to the Côte d'Azur a day later I shared a compartment with a Frenchwoman nursing a baby that yelled all night. I was too preoccupied to mind.

When I arrived in Nice I went to my hotel and rang Blake, arranging to meet him at our agreed rendezvous spot, the Café Massena. It was lunchtime when we met, and within half an hour six or seven of the others joined us. Blake was a bit upset that I had not driven down with him.

"I had to visit a friend in Paris," I told him. "It might save time if we go across to the casino now and pick up our admission cards for tomorrow. Give you all a look at the place."

As we were climbing the stairs inside the casino building I explained that passports would have to be shown. Keith Robinson said he had left his at the hotel. I said he could bring it tomorrow when we started playing. He pulled me back, letting the others go on up.

"What do they want passports for?"

"Just a formality—they check the names against the banned list."

"You sure it's just a formality?"

"Yes. Why?"

He smiled and gave me a wink. "Just wondered, that's all. Never gone much on bureaucracy and red tape and that."

I knew there was more to it than that but said nothing until we had looked round the huge salon of the casino and gone back across the square to the café. When the

others went back to their hotels to get ready for dinner I got him on his own.

"I want to know what's wrong with your passport," I said.

"What do you mean, Norman?"

"I want a straight answer."

He thought about it for a few moments, then became his usual droll self again.

"I can trust you, Norman, can't I? Of course I can. Only I never bothered to get a kosher passport, did I?"

"You mean you're travelling on a false passport?" I snapped.

"Yeah—here it is—not a bad bit of work, is it?"

I didn't bother looking at it.

"What the devil do you need a false passport for? Good God, man, something like this could ruin the whole scheme."

"Don't panic so, Norman. It got me past the immigration and all that crap, didn't it?"

"Just tell me *why.*"

"All right. The fact of it is, Norman, I told you I'm a clerk but actually I'm a burglar."

"You're not serious!"

"Never more. You think burglars look different from normal people?"

"But why the false passport?"

"It's a long story, Norman. I don't think you really want to hear it—I mean, like my name isn't Keith Robinson and so forth? Don't look so sick; I'm not up to anything dodgy. I'll tell you. I saw your ad and thought well, go along, my son, have a bit of a giggle. Maybe give the man's house the once over. Then I got really interested in the scheme. Don't worry. I wouldn't pull any strokes on you. We're all mates in this team, aren't we?"

I took a deep breath.

"It's no business of mine what you say you are. I'm interested only in how you perform at the table. I won't tell anyone else and I presume you don't intend to. Just one thing—keep your hands off the team's money."

"I'm a burglar, remember, not a pickpocket," he said cheerfully.

I had a good few whiskies that night, both with Blake and afterwards on my own. In the end I decided it was too late to worry about Robinson. I needed him and he was reliable, and with only a few hours before our first day's play I was in no position to develop strong moral attitudes. As long as his passport could stand inspection I didn't care if he was the Boston Strangler.

As you will remember from the opening of this account our first day at the Casino Municipale in Nice went extremely well, to the tune of 78,000 francs. Almost six thousand pounds ($15,900). Blake said, as he dropped me back at my hotel after the share-out in his apartments, that it felt too good to be true.

I didn't bother to tell him that the first day was always the easiest.

11

When I awoke on October 1, the second day of our assault on the Casino Municipale, the temperature was in the nineties and the sky blue enough to put an ache in the heart of any sun-starved Briton. After a hearty English-style breakfast I put the shirt and socks I'd worn the day before into the washbasin for a soak, checked that I still had my 7,800 francs from the share-out, and set out through the scorching streets to call on Mrs. Richardson, anxious to hear what had transpired at her cocktail party with the Police des Jeux officer. She had managed to rent a furnished apartment near the casino. Mrs. Harper-Biggs and Mrs. Heppenstall had apartments in another residential building nearby. Apart from Blake with his suite of rooms the rest of us were in pensions and small hotels scattered about the town.

When I arrived it was eleven o'clock and Mrs. Richardson was in her little kitchenette washing clothes. Because of the heat she was wearing only a brassiere and nylon slip. To give her a chance to put some clothes on I said I would have a look round the other room. She didn't feel like bothering. Her streaked blond hair was tied severely back in a ponytail. Standing with her bare arms deep in

the suds, her eyes slightly screwed up against smoke from the cigarette stuck in her mouth, she presented a strangely attractive picture. It was hard to believe she had three sons at boarding school.

"You like this place?" she asked, draining the sink and spreading out a pair of panties on the window ledge.

"Very pleasant. What—"

"I had to fork out a month's rent in advance—a hundred and forty pounds. Still, it means I can save money cooking for myself and I can have a bath whenever I feel like it."

"That will be convenient for you," I said, smiling at the idea of her and the Brigadier having to worry about saving a few pounds. "What happened at the cocktail party?"

"It was interesting," she said, putting on a kettle. "Philippe either fancies me or he's on to us—he stuck by me all night."

"What did he actually say?"

"The usual sort of things. What was I doing here on my own, how long was I staying, was I married? I said my husband and I always took separate holidays—to keep the magic in our marriage. They're so old-fashioned, Frenchmen—he found the very idea shocking. He asked me if I'd come here to gamble. I said I didn't know much about gambling and casinos but had always rather fancied myself raking in piles of chips. I thought I'd pump him for a bit. I said I'd read in the papers that a gang of Australian conmen were working in casinos along the Riviera —did people like that make much money? He said his people were already on to the Australians. He said it's impossible to put one over on the casinos. He started showing off a bit. You know how silly men can be. I couldn't imagine *you* being silly like that—you're always so precise and formal."

"I find it helps to inspire confidence."

"What are you really like then?"

"I can't remember."

"Smile more. It will give people a clue when you're joking."

"I've had this obsession with roulette most of my adult life and in the process I've probably become—well, almost mechanical. Making this system work in this casino is more important to me than anything else, even my wife. I'm sorry, but please don't expect me to be the life and soul of the party. What else did your friend tell you?"

"He was showing off, so I did my empty-headed-blonde act and pumped him like mad. Do you know they have a special group of expert croupiers they can call in when anybody is doing too well? Seemingly these chaps can make the ball finish up wherever they want on the wheel. Not in any particular number—he says that's impossible—but they can put it in whatever section they want. Do you think that's likely?"

"I must think about that. Anyway, I'll wander round to Blake's hotel now."

"He's gone swimming. Peter Vincent is driving to Cap Ferrat, and Maurice Nathan is inspecting the delights of the maritime museum."

"You're very well informed."

"I've never had so many invitations in one morning. The concierge was a bit miffed with all the running up and down to the phone."

"Blake as well? Vincent yes, even Nathan I suppose—but *Blake*? I thought he was engaged to some well-bred filly from the county stable. Well, well."

"It was only for a swim. Good God, I'm an old married woman with three sons."

As she said this she was standing in the doorway of her bedroom, still wearing the white bra and flimsy slip, the

sun behind her in the bedroom window. She had the silhouette of a ripe seventeen-year-old.

"You might carry snapshots of your boys to show around," I said. "Help to remind everybody that you're an old married woman."

When we met at the pavement tables of the Café Massena at two, I told the others what Mrs. Richardson had learned from her police admirer.

"It took the Regency staff eight days to fathom out what method we were using," I said. "You can take it the staff here is much more professional. Once we have been identified and they have discovered our method there are many ways they can put pressure on us, so let's try to keep one jump ahead. Don't let anyone see what you're writing in your notepad. I'm inclined to believe your police friend was telling the truth, Emma. In a gaming industry of this size nothing would be left to chance. I want you to watch for any new faces among the croupiers. From now on you must place your stakes on the table only *after* the tourneur has thrown the ball. I'm not saying the game will be rigged, but the longer we keep them in the dark the better. You'll all be covering the same chances as yesterday. By the way, where's Mr. Sherlock?"

"He's asked me to take his turn this afternoon and he'll do mine tonight," said Keith Robinson, who was wearing new and expensive sunglasses.

"Something wrong with him?"

"He's got a bit of a headache, hasn't he?"

"Well?" said Blake coldly. "Has he or hasn't he?"

Robinson turned his dark glasses in Blake's direction. "I just told you he had, didn't I?"

"We had a drop of champagne last night at the hotel," Terry Baker said.

Robinson groaned theatrically, "More'n a drop. We didn't get to bed till eight this morning, did we?"

"What you mean is that Sherlock is too drunk to get out of bed," Blake snapped. Robinson turned the dark glasses on him once more.

"You could say that, Olly old boy," he said slowly and with more than a hint of menace, "if it was any of your business."

I intervened before Blake could react to what was clearly a challenge. "I don't care in the least what you all do in your spare time but I must insist on being consulted before anyone changes shifts."

"I could go back and roust him out of his pit," Robinson said.

"No, if he's under the weather he'd go through hell this afternoon in there," I said. "The heat will be fantastic."

"May I put in a word, Mr. Leigh?" said Blake, dressed despite the temperature in his usual rig-out of heavy blue pinstripe suit, with waistcoat, stiff white collar and tightly knotted Old Etonian tie. I wondered if he had enjoyed the rampant informality of the beach. "From our experiences in the Regency I'd say that casinos prefer to harass a winning team and provoke incidents that give them the excuse of bad behaviour for banning people. I'd suggest we make doubly sure we are on our best behaviour and avoid *any* kind of incident."

"I agree. And under no circumstances allow yourselves to be questioned by the staff without either Mr. Blake or myself being present. Well now, two forty-five. Shall we go across?"

Walking across the square in blinding sunshine, I caught up with Robinson.

"You seem a bit tetchy with Blake," I said quietly. "I hope you're not letting his little mannerisms rub you up the wrong way."

"Every time he opens his bloody mouth he gives me a pain."

"He can't help the way he speaks."

"Go on, nobody talks like that for real."

"For Christ's sake, if you're going to be foolish enough to develop a phobia about Blake and the way he talks, you're going to ruin this team's chances of success and lose us all a lot of money. Pull yourself together!"

"Yes, you're right. I'll feel better once this hangover's gone. Expensive down here, innit? I think we were paying ten quid a bottle for the bubbly."

"It's one of the most expensive places in the world."

"Sure is: even if you win you still lose."

As we stepped out of the blinding sunshine into the shade of the casino stairway I said to Mrs. Harper-Biggs and Mrs. Heppenstall that if they found the heat too much I would arrange to have them relieved for a rest.

"*Heat?*" said Mrs. Harper-Biggs, who was wearing her usual tweeds and carrying a string bag big enough to hold a large dog. "I don't call this heat. Herbert and I spent some years in the Belgian Congo; *that's* what I call heat, Mr. Leigh."

"I bought myself a new summer dress this morning," said Mrs. Heppenstall with a guilty little giggle.

"Yes, Lettice and I went on a *most* extravagant shopping spree," said Mrs. Harper-Biggs.

"I daresay we'll be hearing next that you've both been on champagne binges," I remarked.

The little widow from Hastings looked shocked. "Oh, Mr. Leigh! As if we would!"

The salon was fairly busy, the usual mixture, aged relics of bygone days stalking among the genuinely affluent of many nationalities, here and there groups of curious tourists nervously building up courage for a flutter. The first shift came to the table in twos and threes, trying to create as little attention as possible among the other players. Once they were seated I had a quiet word with Blake.

"Be careful not to let any tension build up between you and Robinson," I said. "It's up to you and me to handle everybody with tact. We're operating at the bare minimum and we can't afford the risk of losing anyone through heavy-handedness."

"If we let slackness creep in we may lose the whole lot," he replied stiffly. "What are you going to do about Sherlock?"

"I'll have a word with him. He did make sure he had a replacement."

"You don't think some sort of fine would be in order?"

"If I thought he was going to let me down, I'd suggest a good flogging, but this isn't the Foreign Legion."

It took a couple of hours before anything happened that second afternoon. Keith Robinson had the beginnings of a progression on black, but it petered out before his line produced stakes in the hundreds. (The exchange rate at that time was approximately 13.7 new francs to the pound (4.94 francs to the dollar); the table minimum was 5 francs and the maximum, on even chances, 2,600 francs (£190—$525).

Half an hour later black again began to predominate over red by slightly more than 2 to 1. As his staking calculations began to involve him in four-digit additions he kept licking his lips and frowning. Time and time again his scribbled calculations gave him the amount he had to stake with just enough time to grab the right selection of plaques and chips. He had not been playing long enough in the Casino Municipale to know automatically which colours of plaques and chips represented different values. Adding sums like 179 and 1,554 is not difficult in normal circumstances, but at the table the seconds are racing towards the next play and those figures represent real money to be won or lost depending on how accurate you are.

Besides watching over Robinson's shoulder I also had

to keep an eye on Mrs. Harper-Biggs, who was showing signs of being in trouble. Normally a roulette table has nine or ten players seated and perhaps another twenty standing. As the news of Keith's winning progression spread through the salon more people began to congregate at our table. As Keith started piling up the plaques and chips the crowd grew thicker, pressing closer to see what he was betting on. Some even tried to count the exact number of chips he was staking so that they, too, could stake the same amount and thereby, they hoped, be brushed by the magic of success.

By the time Keith's progression had taken him to stakes of above 1,000 francs there must have been a hundred people jammed round the table. Once again we heard the slow rhythm of the coded handclaps as the croupiers alerted officials in other parts of the large salon. Black came up three times in succession. His stakes rose, nearing the table limit of 2,600 francs. People pushed and craned from the back to get a glimpse of the action.

"The temperature must be into the hundreds in here," Blake said, perspiration forming on his forehead and his pale, fleshy cheeks.

"I think Mrs. Harper-Biggs is looking a bit shaky too," I said.

"If she faints, I'll take over her chair," said Blake. I realized with some slight sense of surprise that I had been worrying more about Mrs. Harper-Biggs herself than about missing a few spins.

She did not faint, however, and at 5:45 P.M. the Chef de Partie, the table supervisor, had to announce that play was stopping temporarily at this table.

"He's broken the table," Blake said excitedly. "I take back all I said about him."

Keith sat there calmly sorting out his winnings while the crowd stared at him. Those nearest asked him what

system he had been using. He gave them cheery little winks, lifting the 1,000- and 500-franc plaques into his jacket pockets.

With an interval of around twenty minutes before fresh reserves of chips and plaques could be brought to the table the crowd began to dissipate, and I picked up Keith's notepad to see what he had won. There were too many uncrossed figures to add up in my head.

"It looks like something around sixty thousand francs," I said to him.

He nodded, giving Blake a knowing smile. "Should be enough for a few magnums there, eh, *Oliver?*"

Blake managed a smile.

One person who did not drift away from the table during the lull was my old friend the Chef de Casino, the director of the establishment. He stood behind the tourneur eyeing Keith thoughtfully.

When play started again the crowd returned to see more fireworks. But what was there now to see? Keith had pocketed his winnings and had written 1, 2, 3, 4 in the top left-hand corner of a fresh page in his pad. What excitement was there in watching someone bet 5 miserable francs?

The second shift began arriving between eight and nine. Moving far enough from the table to avoid being overheard, I beckoned Alec Sherlock over. He looked uneasy.

"Look," I said, "I don't care how drunk you get at night but I must remind you of the group's rules. If you think you'd prefer to be on the second shift, I'll switch you over and you can sleep all afternoon."

"That would be better actually," he said. "I'm sorry about—"

"These things can happen to anyone. You're due to cover black—better get in position behind Keith now.

With a crowd like that we'll lose the seats if we aren't spot on."

"Yes, okay. There's just one thing—could you lend me some money?"

"I shouldn't leave it lying about your hotel room. Or have you posted it home already? I should keep—"

"No, I haven't done that."

"You mean you—but you had four hundred pounds from the share-out last night!"

"I was a fool," he said, shuddering.

"What happened?"

"Well, Keith and Terry and I had a few drinks in the hotel and these girls appeared and—oh God. I was as drunk as a lord. When I woke up this morning she was gone and so was the money."

"*All* of it?" He nodded. "Well, who was she? The hotel staff must know her. Ordinarily I'd tell you to write it off as experience, but four hundred pounds is too expensive a lesson. The police—"

"She didn't steal it. I gave it to her."

"You did *what?*"

Blake came up and tapped my elbow. "I think Mrs. Richardson is on to something," he said.

"I'll be with you in a moment." I waited until he was out of range. "I'll lend you two hundred francs. You'd better cure yourself of these generous impulses."

"Don't worry. I've learned my lesson, Norman," he said fervently.

I went back to the table. Mrs. Richardson was into a sequence where red predominated over black by roughly 5 to 2. It was one of those progressions which showed little initial promise, always threatening to peter out and then coming to life again when she had only two uncrossed figures on her line and one more loss would have sent her back to 1, 2, 3, 4.

No longer the half-clad girlish figure of our morning tête-à-tête but wearing the black cocktail dress she kept for casino work, she looked incredibly attractive. Possibly the best arithmetician in the group, she could do all her calculations without writing them down and always had time to spare for her selection of chips. The more she won the more relaxed she became.

She had been sitting at the table for six hours and forty minutes when she came near the limit of 2,600 francs. Peter Vincent should have taken over her chair at 9 P.M., but I had told him not to break into her progression.

Again we had the complete paraphernalia, the agitated curiosity of the chattering crowd, the softly insistent hand-clapping of the croupiers, the arrival of the senior staff, the unemotional calls of the tourneur—and then, the moment which always floored staff and spectators alike, the moment that was so crucial to our success and which so mystified everyone else, when she crossed out the line of figures she had been working on, turned to a new page, wrote 1, 2, 3, 4, selected a pink 5-franc chip and placed it on the section of the green baize marked red.

She had reached the limit and won, at the subsequent count, 39,375 francs—£2,800 ($8,000)!

"In you go," I said to Vincent. Mrs. Richardson rose, and he eased into her place before any of those crowded behind realized a switch was taking place.

I went with her to the cash desk, Blake being at the table by then with the second shift. She was as fresh as the dew, but I had been on my feet since 3 P.M. When she suggested I go with her and the other two ladies, Lettice and Cynthia (Mrs. Harper-Biggs' other name, it appeared), to her apartment for coffee, I was tempted to call it a day.

It was as well I did decide to stick it out until close of play at 3 A.M. Hopplewell had been having one of

those frustrating sessions which rarely got beyond stakes of 20 francs. As quickly as he wrote down a fresh line of 1, 2, 3, 4 the wheel went against him and he had to cross the line out and start again.

At 1:30 A.M., when only the obsessed and the insomniac remained at the tables besides the eternally bland and tireless staff, the wheel began to run for him. He was betting on *pair*, the even numbers. The ball began to fall in even numbers three times to every once it landed in an odd number.

His mushroom went fairly quickly. This time, however, with fewer people in the casino, there was not such a crowd round the table and when the inevitable ritual of the coded handclaps drew what seemed like the entire management to his table there seemed to be more staff present than patrons.

"I have a distinct feeling they're ready to take steps against us," Blake said to me without looking round. I looked at my watch.

"They'll have to look sharp about it," I said. "There's only half an hour to go." I saw Hopplewell saying something quickly to a waiter between spins. In a few minutes the waiter reappeared and set a brandy glass down beside his pile of winning plaques and chips. "Likes a brandy, does our Mr. Hopplewell," Blake muttered. "You know that's his seventh since we sat down?"

"Hardly more than one an hour, is it? Doesn't seem to be affecting him much."

Blake placed a stake of 76 francs on red. It lost, and he deleted the last two figures of that sequence. Hopplewell had won, however. Brandy glass in his left hand, he did his paperwork with his right hand and then frowned. He was too tired on this occasion to think of showing off. I saw him drag the pen through his page of figures. He had reached the limit.

He and the other five played out the last few spins and

then it was all over for another day. We went to the cash desk. Hopplewell had won 33,125 francs.

"My God, I feel as if I've been down the mines for a fortnight," Milton groaned. "The only thing that could revive me right now is a large Scotch."

"The sight of the loot's my tonic," said Keith Robinson, who had come back to the casino after eating. "How much did we take the frogs for today, Oliver?"

Onto Blake's Georgian dining table dropped the wads of French currency. "It seems to come to one hundred and thirty thousand four hundred and fifty francs," Blake said.

Robinson squinted at the notes. "Very colourful," he said. "Who's the geezers they've got here instead of the Queen?"

"That's Pascal," I said, pointing to a 500-franc note. "Ironically enough, some historians believe he started roulette. He was a philosopher investigating the laws of chance with a cartwheel in his yard, spinning it to see where it stopped. He had to stop work when it rained so he had a miniature wheel made for indoor work. The other one is Cardinal Richelieu."

Keith looked at me and nodded approvingly. "Pascal the rascal, eh? Did us a good turn, didn't he, brainy old bastard."

Blake began to write in his cash book. Like everything else about him his numerals were almost painfully neat and correct.

Vincent yawned and said, "About ten thousand pounds, isn't it?"

Blake pointedly ignored this statement. Eventually he looked up and said, "It's nine thousand five hundred and twenty-one pounds with about eight francs left over [$26,600]."

"I never was any good at maths," Vincent drawled.

Blake again ignored him determinedly. Reading from his cash book, he said that he and I were due 13,045 francs each and that the balance of 104,360 francs split eleven ways produced a share of 9,487 francs each, or £690 ($1,930).

Vincent, Hopplewell, Sherlock, Milton, Robinson, Fredericks, and I each took a wad of francs from Blake, who then filled a white envelope for each of those who had preferred to turn in. It was now 4 A.M.

"I thought we might all have a snort or two to mark our success," Blake said stiffly. Whether he liked Vincent or not, good form decreed that the invitation should include everybody.

"I've never been one for stag parties much, ducks," said Vincent, drooping a queenly wrist and then mincing across the room to the door.

"Did you say something about a brandy?" Hopplewell asked gruffly, when he had gone.

"Yes, of course." Blake produced a bottle of five-star and some glasses from the cocktail cabinet. As he was pouring Hopplewell remarked: "Damned hot in there today." Blake handed him his glass. He drank it all and held the glass out. "Bad for the throat, smoky atmosphere like that," he grunted, leaving Blake little option but to pour him a refill.

"Couldn't one of us tactfully suggest to Mrs. Harper-Biggs that she might wear something a little more suited to this climate," Fredericks said. "Poor old thing was near to fainting this afternoon."

"I'll mention it to Emma," I said.

"It's the damned smoke, gets in your chest," said Hopplewell, coughing and tapping his throat.

"There's one thing strikes me," said Milton. "It was the same in the Regency—what really gets their goats, those casino wallahs, is not so much that we win a lot

of money. It's the way we immediately go back to one, two, three, four. That really sickens them."

"I quite enjoy watching their faces when we have a mushroom," said Fredericks, beaming gleefully, clearly just beginning to realize he did not have to apologize for his existence.

"Yes, it is a bit strong," said Robinson. "I mean, one minute we're taking them for thousands of francs, next we're putting on a measly five. We ought to put on a few silly bets just to give them some of the loot back."

"No, seriously," said Milton, "it does ram it down their throats a bit."

Hopplewell made a few coughing noises. "Must do something to clear this up," he said, reaching for the brandy bottle. "Don't mind, do you, Blake?"

He was already pouring when Blake said no, of course not, by all means, at the same time glancing at me meaningfully. Hopplewell sat down. His face looked slightly bluish, but that could have been the light. He didn't seem drunk.

"Is there any way we could make the drop in stakes less obvious?" said Sherlock.

"I'm afraid not," I said, "apart from deliberately throwing away money as Keith suggested. Stopping as soon as the progression reaches the limit is the linchpin of the whole scheme. We only bet when the percentages suit us and we don't give them a chance to win the money back."

"Forgive my stupidity, but could you tell me again why it is exactly we have to go back to a five-franc bet as soon as we reach the limit or break the table?" Fredericks asked. I was astonished that he had come this far without grasping the point.

"The method depends on the ability to increase your bets while you're winning," I said as patiently as possible. "If we carried on betting at the limit, the table would

have an even chance of winning the money back without our being able to compensate with higher bets. Suppose you have two thousand pounds in front of you after a long upwards progression. If you go on betting at two thousand pounds, you immediately cease to be a system player—you're exactly in the position of a man who comes to the table with two thousand pounds and starts betting on an even chance at the maximum. Would you do that with two thousand of your own money?"

"Yes, but we're not risking our own money. All that two thousand has just come from the table."

"Exactly. And we want to keep it, don't we? The seeds of our own destruction lie within all of us. The system safeguards us against our own human weaknesses. Study the case history of any compulsive gambler and you will see the pattern—he starts with a big win and spends or ruins the rest of his life trying to recapture that magic moment. Left to ourselves without a rigid frame of rules we would all succumb to temptation. Win two thousand and we want to make it four. Lose two thousand and we would try to win it back, and lose another two thousand in the process. The system *forces* us to be clever, to give up while we are ahead. Do you think you've grasped it now?"

"Yes," said Fredericks, no doubt wishing he had never opened his mouth. Hopplewell made some chesty noises and reached for the brandy bottle. Blake wasted no time with subtle hints but stood up and said it was time he drove me to my hotel. Hopplewell pretended that he had only picked up the bottle to read the label. "Good stuff that," he said. "Must get some for my cough."

We all left Blake's hotel and said our farewells on the pavement in the comparatively cool air of predawn.

As soon as Blake and I were alone in his Sunbeam Alpine he said, "I have no doubt we shall be banned within the next forty-eight hours."

"Why do you say that?"

"Did you see their faces when we left tonight? They were positively malevolent."

"They'll think hard before they ban us merely for winning, especially a government-run municipal casino. Wouldn't be good for business."

"Do you think they'll worry about their public relations if they go on losing ten thousand pounds a day? I think not."

"If they ban us, they ban us, and that will be that. As long as we have committed no crime—"

"We have committed the unpardonable crime of being successful. By the way, Hopplewell was punishing the brandy in no uncertain fashion."

"Doesn't seem to have much effect on him."

"That might be a bad sign. Know much about the man?"

"Not a great deal. He owns several companies. I don't know what line he's in."

"Looks prosperous enough. Wonder why he joined a scheme like this."

"He told me it was purely a business speculation— he hates gambling, he said. Come to that, why did you join?"

He hesitated, sensing the dangerous currents of personal intimacy. I was too tired to care. It wasn't until we were outside my hotel that he turned towards me with some deliberation.

"Back there in my digs—I think that was the single most satisfying moment of my life. Would you really like to know why I came on this trip?"

Groaning inwardly at my own stupidity, I closed the door again and prepared for the stiff upper lip to pour out repressed emotions.

"I suppose it sounds rather vulgar but obviously I do not need this money." After a short but awkward silence

he went on: "Perhaps that's wrong. I don't need money as such, but I do need *this* money. Does that make sense?"

"Not exactly."

"I've had money all my life. Born into the stuff; never been without it. Nothing but Eton was good enough for *my* father's son. Eton, Oxford—I even had a year at Harvard. Straight into the family firm. Easy progress to the day when I would take over—hard work of course but many, many compensations. People like to say money has its own problems—generally people with no money. I've never found any problems. Quite the reverse. It's too easy, life, if you have money. Look, you may not believe this, but that money we shared out—it's given me more satisfaction than anything else in my whole life. I mean it. It didn't come through my father or my accent or my Eton connections. No, I made it in a venture where none of that counted, something my father had no hand in. Not that I dislike the—"

"I understand," I said, wondering if his invitation to swim with Mrs. Richardson indicated another area in which he wished to prove his independence.

October 2, our third day; temperature 90 degrees Fahrenheit. I spent the morning sitting outside a café near my hotel, having a dry martini before buying a packet of envelopes and stamps for sending home some of the 21,000 francs (approximately £1,500—$4,200) I had won in these first two days. Life seemed very good, sitting in the sun. Pauline was coming down as soon as she could get on a flight, probably tomorrow. At last she would see that I was making the wild dream work.

I had seen the corpulent man in the pink shirt and dark glasses walk past the café but had taken no great interest in him at the time. Then I saw him stop, turn round and come back through the tables towards me.

"Monsieur, may I introduce myself?" he said. "My name is Charles Berteille. I have seen you and your friends at the casino."

"Have you?" I said, pleasantly enough.

"May I sit with you? Forgive my intrusion." He snapped finger and thumb to attract a waiter. "Would Monsieur like—"

"No, thank you."

He ordered cognac. "I am from Perpignan. I own a small factory," he said. I nodded. Leaning across the table, he said in a much lower voice, "I have been gambling in the casino for three months and you and your friends are the first people I have seen winning with such regularity. Amazing."

"Yes, we've been rather lucky."

"Lucky?" He leaned even closer. "Are you moving from casino to casino or is your intention to concentrate on the Casino Municipale here?"

"Why do you ask?"

"Have you ever thought of what happens to people who win large sums from a casino with consistency?"

"They get rich, I suppose."

"Perhaps. There is a book you should read, by a German baron. He has evidence that over the years numbers of people have disappeared both here on the Côte d'Azur and in Monte Carlo. The common denominator in their disappearance was that they had been winning large sums of money over a long period."

"Perhaps they were tired of their wives."

"You always joke, you English. I was in London through the war. I have many good English friends. That is why I wanted to speak to you when I saw you sitting here. You are already well known in this town, monsieur, you and your friends, especially the young men who hold the wild parties."

"Must be some other people you're thinking of," I

said. "My friends are very respectable, no wild parties."

"No?" He examined my face, then shrugged. Drinking his cognac in the precise French way, he put down the glass and looked at me again.

"Wonderful weather for October," I said.

"You may laugh at me, monsieur, but because I like the English so much I want to warn you. You should listen."

"I must say, you speak English quite well," I said pleasantly. He went off abruptly, apparently insulted. I paid my *addition* and went back to the hotel.

It took me half an hour to address eight or nine envelopes. Each contained three or four 100-franc notes or one 500-franc note, folded into sheets of blank notepaper. I posted these in different boxes and had lunch on my own. It was 2:40 P.M. when I arrived at the Café Massena. The first shift was preparing to cross the square to the casino. They all seemed in good spirits. Fredericks said he had noticed that the players here tipped the croupiers a good deal more than in the Regency.

"I object to tipping them in principle," I said, "but it probably makes them more congenial. No more than forty francs, though, and only at the end of your shift."

"They do seem very friendly and helpful," said Mrs. Heppenstall. "They must be very clever: all those people putting down chips on different numbers yet they never make mistakes, do they? I could never remember which players put on all those different stakes."

"They're highly trained—they have to be. But don't make the mistake of regarding them as your friends."

"Are they—you know—gigolos?" Mrs. Heppenstall asked timidly.

"Don't fall for one of them if that's what you mean," I said sternly. "You may well find yourself involved with the fringes of criminal life."

"Oh, Mr. Leigh! As if I ever would!"

I patted her on the shoulder and said we would keep an eye on her nevertheless.

We had to wait only thirty minutes for the first progression to appear. Hopplewell had asked for a switch to the first shift because, he alleged, he preferred to get to bed before dawn. He had taken over black from Sherlock, who had moved to the second shift.

(The first shift in full consisted of Mrs. Richardson, on red; Hopplewell, black; Mrs. Heppenstall, *pair* (even); Mrs. Harper-Biggs, *impair* (odd); Maurice Nathan, *manque* (low); George Milton, *passe* (high). Covering these chances in the same order for the second shift were Blake, Fredericks, Sherlock, Robinson, Vincent and Baker.)

In something like sixty-two spins Hopplewell was getting very near the table limit of 2,600 francs. He had been chasing this progression for two hours (the longest time span of the progressions we had had so far had been about three hours, the shortest an hour). His progress had been accompanied by the usual handclapping, the gathering of an excited crowd and the stern attentions of the senior staff, though not, on this occasion, those of the tireless Chef de Casino.

Hopplewell's line read 285, 360, 435, 526, 633, 740, 847, 978, 1,109, 1,240, 1,399, 1,554, 1,709, 1,864, 2,043, 2,222. His next bet would have been 285 + 2,222—2,507, which was a bare 93 francs below the maximum stake. This line of figures of course represented winning bets, which meant that he had plaques and chips worth about 18,000 francs piled up in front of him on the green baize.

One more win would have taken him over the limit— and produced total winnings for the progression of over 20,000 francs, approximately £1,500 ($4,000).

The wheel, however, decided to tantalize him and his

next bet did not win. He scored out the figures at either end of the line. His next stake was 360 + 2,043—2,403 francs. It lost as well. Again he had to score out the end figures. With stakes of that size it does not take too many losing bets for the accumulated winnings to start shrinking. Having favoured black for two hours, the wheel developed a strong preference for red. While this looked as though it might wipe out Hopplewell's profits it naturally gave Mrs. Richardson the beginnings of a mushroom, which was, of course, the great strength of playing as a team covering all the even chances simultaneously. The wheel does not often throw up a sequence long enough to take a player to the table limit (once every six days, I had worked out), but when it does a team of six acting as a collective unit must reap the profits.

On the other hand, every scientific law states quite categorically that each spin is a random event entirely disconnected from all previous and all future spins. Hopplewell had gone a long way on a sequence which favoured his chance, black, but just as the finishing tape was in sight it looked as if all his winnings were to be taken back. Why did he not stop betting as soon as he felt that his luck had run out and save some of the winnings? Because we were playing to a strictly ordained method; allow each player to exert individual choice based on a feeling or a hunch and the whole thing would have collapsed.

Hopplewell's next stake was 435 + 1,864—2,299. As he was putting it on I listened to a conversation between an elderly Frenchman and two younger men whom I took to be his sons. He was explaining what Hopplewell was doing, and I was surprised to realize that despite all precautionary measures—hiding what was on the notepads and placing stakes at the last moment—this man had grasped completely the staking principle of the Reverse Labouchère.

Hopplewell lost again. His line now read 526, 633, 740, 847, 978, 1,109, 1,240, 1,399, 1,554, 1,709. His next stake was, therefore, 526 + 1,709—2,235.

This time he won. His next stake would have been 526 + 2,235—2,761, over the limit. That little adverse sequence at the end had more or less halved his winnings, which were, if you care to add up that last list of figures, 10,735 francs.

As soon as he had scored out that page and written 1, 2, 3, 4 in the corner of the next sheet of his pad, Hopplewell began to look round in an anxious fashion.

"Is there something wrong?" I asked him.

"Oh yes," he said, patting his chest and giving a few rasping coughs. "Can you see a bloody waiter, my throat's terrible."

Looking round for a waiter, I caught sight of Blake. He came as near as the crowd permitted, and I asked him to order a large brandy for Hopplewell. When I turned back to the table I saw that the spotlight had fallen on George Milton. He was getting a predominance on *passe* (the numbers nineteen to thirty-six on the wheel) of 3 to 1. Paradoxically, too many wins at the early stage of a progression are something of a handicap; if you start with 1, 2, 3, 4 and keep winning three times to every once that you lose it takes a long time for the stake to get into three figures. If you start with 1, 2, 3, 4 and win your first twenty consecutive bets, these low figures are never deleted, and each stake increases by only one unit. Ideally what you want are just enough wins to keep the line from being deleted altogether at the early stages, a predominance of 5 to 2 or 7 to 3 in your favour. By spin 22 you may have a line that reads 16, 24, 34, 50. That means forty-five minutes in which you have won 124 units. However, you have got rid of the smallest numbers, and if you go on enjoying a 5 to 2 predominance, the stakes will begin to mushroom quite quickly. Then,

ideally, you want the last lap of the progression to coincide with a greater predominance in your favour—3 to 1 being ideal. This means you finish with a fair number of winning bets at high stakes.

It was about half-past five when Milton's staking progression brought him to the limit. He had won 21,680 francs. Back he went to 1, 2, 3, 4. From what I could see over the heads of those crowded round the table the rest of the salon was pretty well deserted. I looked for the Chef de Casino and saw him standing beside the Chef de Partie, his face impassive.

Around 6:45 P.M. Mrs. Richardson went into a progression on red. This one lasted well over two hours. Although she was on the other side of the table from where I was standing, with her left hand shielding her notepad from prying eyes, I could follow her staking pattern well enough to know that it was one of those mushrooms which continually look like petering out. That meant her line was often reduced to only two figures before another sequence of wins brought it back to life. These slow ones often won most in the end, if they lasted.

This one did. Shortly before the shifts were due to change over the Chef de Partie announced that the table was closing temporarily. Mrs. Richardson had broken it. A complete hush fell on the mob round the table. As she began to put the large plaques into her handbag Mrs. Richardson might have been on a stage in front of a silently engrossed theater audience. Nobody moved. I kept my eyes on the Chef de Casino.

For a few long seconds he stood there motionless. Then he said something to the tourneur. The message was passed to the croupier. No announcement was made, but the table staff left their posts.

"Are they going to bring more chips?" Mrs. Richardson asked me when I moved round the table.

"It doesn't look like it. You did very well there."

"Funny, you hardly notice the crowd and the hand-clapping after a while. Where has all the glamour gone? I feel that I'm just doing a job."

"That's good. Let's have a look at your figures and we'll see how much you've won."

"I've added them already. It's thirty-three thousand, seven hundred and fifty francs. By the way, I heard one of those bigwigs saying something about tabulating our results—it was time they started tabulating our results. What would that mean?"

"They want to know exactly how we're working. It's an obvious move."

An announcement was then made that our table had been closed for the day. Everybody had to move to another table. In the general confusion only Mrs. Harper-Biggs and Mrs. Heppenstall were lucky enough to get seats. Mrs. Richardson told us later how it felt to stand.

"That was really like hard work. I honestly hoped I wouldn't get a progression because it would have been so difficult to concentrate with all those people jostling around—my handbag with my chips in one hand, trying to do my paperwork with my pad balanced on my arm. I won't be wearing such high heels when I'm playing in future, that's a certainty."

The fact was that she had shown more guts than most men I had known. Like the rest of the group she had very little previous experience at roulette and therefore had no idea just how arduous a task they were being asked to perform. I have known scores of alleged devotees of the game who regard a couple of hours at the table as hard work. Even then they are liable to become bored and start playing single numbers on hunches to break what they call the "monotony." What I required of my twelve players was that they become professional rou-

lette players in the strict sense of the word—instantly. If they had spent more time in casinos, they would have realized how much I was asking of them. I did not feel any purpose would be served by bringing this to their attention—it isn't the narrowness of the tightrope that upsets the balance but the drop below. My little band was walking the tightrope blindfold and nobody had told them that it was impossible.

Blake was coming from the bar when he noticed a group of smartly dressed men having words with the Chef de Casino. He pointed them out to me. It was obvious they were discussing us.

"Who do you think they are?" he asked.

"Officials of some description. They can stand there and discuss us all night for all I care."

"I met Vincent down at the seafront this afternoon," said Blake. "He had some girl in tow. It's difficult to get much out of him, but he did tell me that Robinson and Baker and Sherlock are becoming a bit of a public scandal in this town. Did you know that they're throwing *orgies?*"

"Baker—throwing orgies?" I said. "I can hardly believe that. He's been posting his winnings home—he told me that anyway."

"I should press him harder on that score. Hasn't he got a wife and young child?"

"Yes, they're due to join him down here in a day or two. My wife is arriving tomorrow. I think we should have a serious chat after play finishes tonight."

We had no more progressions that day. While Blake was cashing up at the desk I got hold of Terry Baker and suggested we walk to Blake's hotel so that we could have a little chat.

It was a ten-minute walk. At first he stuck to his story that he had been sending most of his winnings home. I said I wondered who then was paying for the champagne

parties I had been hearing about. He said that he and Alec Sherlock and Keith Robinson had been having a bottle or two of champagne once the casino had closed, that was all.

"And when is your wife arriving?"

"I'm phoning her in the morning. The baby had a bit of a temperature when I last called her, but if it clears up she's flying down the day after tomorrow."

"Just as well, possibly."

"What do you mean?"

"It won't cost me any sleep one way or the other, but if you don't come out of this with a reasonable amount of money, it will all have been a dreadful mistake, won't it?"

"I don't know what you're on about," he said heatedly. "I've spent a few quid, but we're making plenty, aren't we? No point in pulling a stroke like this if we've got to live like monks, is there?"

"It's your life."

At the meeting I said that the casino management obviously knew now that they had a problem on their hands and that we should stay alert for any form of provocation designed to foment incidents.

"I should also bear in mind that these casinos come under the auspices of the French government. Indirectly we are challenging the state. I want to remind you all that we are in a foreign country and one whose civilized approach to life goes hand in hand with a certain brutal logic as far as threats to its interests are concerned. If they can't find an excuse to bar us from the casino they might try to find evidence for classifying us as undesirable aliens. I should be extremely careful of the company you keep."

"Yeah, there's lots of thieves and villains about," said Keith Robinson, giving me a wink. "So, how's about divvying up the lolly, Olly—sorry, Oliver."

Blake gave his daily treasurer's report. The total winnings from three progressions were 66,165 francs. He and I had 6,616 francs each (£482–$1,350), leaving 52,933 francs to be split eleven ways, a share each of 4,812 francs (£350–$982).

As soon as they had the money in their hands Robinson, Sherlock and Baker were off. Blake asked the rest of us to stay for a coffee or a brandy. I preferred some exercise.

"I think I'll get some fresh air into my lungs. Fancy a walk, Emma?"

Walking through the quiet streets in the soft Mediterranean night Mrs. Richardson and I decided to have a glass of wine at a bistro. We sat at a table by the open door. She lit a Disque Bleu.

"Changed your brand, I see," I said.

The waiter brought us two glasses and a bottle of Châteauneuf du Pape.

"Can't get mine down here," she said. "Still, these are cheap enough."

"I'm glad the money isn't going to your head. I wish I could say the same about some of the others."

"You mean the three musketeers?" She blew smoke at the ceiling.

"If they want to make fools of themselves, they are perfectly welcome. My only concern is that they ruin the whole thing for everybody else by getting in trouble."

"I think Terry's feeling guilty, but he doesn't want the other two to think he's a goody-goody. They had another swing-ding last night. Keith was boasting that he spent three hundred pounds on champagne alone. And Alec Sherlock—women? You'd think he'd just found out women existed."

"I don't care what they do as long as they turn up on time and stay sober enough to play the system."

"Alec Sherlock is a real surprise. Would you have guessed he would turn out to be—well, what do *you* call it?"

"Sex mad? Perhaps he wasn't until we came down here. Interesting the way various people react when money starts flowing in."

"It makes me quite angry. If I wasn't a respectable old married woman, I might try to get them to squander some of it on me."

"Ah yes, the old married woman. More wine? Lovely night, isn't it? Strange thing about money. Those who've never had it and need it most spend it fastest, while those who're used to it like Blake and yourself and—"

"I hope you're not classing me with Blake!"

"You know what I mean, people who have money—"

"Norman, you've got it all wrong. All this Brigadier nonsense—it is just a joke. You do know that, don't you? Would you like me to tell you what George's last job was?"

"If you want to."

"He was a butler! As a matter of fact he is now an out-of-work butler."

"Really?"

"He wasn't always a butler. He used to run a coffee plantation in Kenya, but after independence there was a big campaign to give Africans the good jobs. Poor George had to come back to an England he hardly knew and didn't like. He was too old to get another job at the same level. He's tried lots of things, but you know how it is. After a lifetime giving orders he finds it hard to take them, especially from jumped-up nobodies who've never been anywhere. Of course I make good money as a commercial designer, but he doesn't like living off me. He even tried to be a film extra! Somebody told him there was a part for a distinguished-looking man to play a butler. He didn't get it, but he said he might as well go the whole

hog and *be* a butler—make a joke out of it. Said it was the only way he could at least still *see* the standard of living he'd been used to. He didn't last long, of course."

"What about your job?"

"I'm a free-lancer. This is my holiday for the year. I can always get plenty of work. You see, what we'd really like to do is buy a small hotel somewhere on the south coast, Chichester maybe. That's why your scheme appealed to us so much, the chance to make some money tax-free. I've been posting it home like mad!"

"Wouldn't it have been more sensible for your husband to play roulette and you to carry on working?"

She shrugged. "He knows himself too well. He wouldn't have been any good in a group effort unless he was the boss. Well, I've given you my secrets. What are yours?"

"I have no secrets."

"Go on, you're one of the cagiest men I've ever known. All this organizing and dedication to take money from this casino? You don't think I haven't noticed that every time somebody asks you what's so special about this casino you change the subject."

"It's very simple. I played here a long time ago with my father and watched him lose every penny we had." I paused, then continued: "And I can still remember the face of the Chef de Casino convulsing himself with laughter."

"I see, revenge."

"Nothing so dramatic. Just remember that I want you and the rest, and *myself*, to be convinced of one thing. I am not an unusually emotional or obsessive man. I have brought us together for rational, cordial, commercial motives and nothing else. Understand?"

She looked at me curiously. "We've only been here a

few days, and already I have the distinct impression that nobody is what I thought they were back in London."

The bottle was finished. "I'll walk you back to your hotel," I said.

When I reached my hotel day had dawned and I was meeting people who had just risen from a decent night's sleep. I felt grey and weary. Two messages had been shoved under my door, one to say that Pauline had phoned and would phone back, the second to say that she had phoned back and would be arriving on the midday flight from London. I got my head down at half-past seven.

Despite the heat I slept soundly until about eleven, when Blake arrived downstairs in a state of some agitation.

12

"I decided to go out for breakfast," Blake said. "I was tucking into a plate of bacon and eggs in one of those small places near the Quay. The bill came to about forty francs. I gave the waiter a five-hundred-franc note—we've been seeing so many of them I'd almost forgotten they were anything out of the ordinary. He still hadn't brought my change after ten minutes, so I went to the cash desk. Suddenly two men appeared and asked me to go with them to the manager's office. Police! They made me sit down and asked me a lot of questions about where I had obtained the five-hundred-franc note. I asked if it were forged, and they said no, but these large notes were being passed all over the town and they wanted to know the source."

"What did you tell them?" I asked, pouring more black coffee.

"What else but the truth? I said I was playing roulette in the Casino Municipale and had been fortunate enough to win substantially. Do you know, one of them more or less called me a liar to my face! That did it as far as I was concerned. I asked if they were charging me with anything. They said no, so I went to the cash desk and demanded my change—then simply walked out. Do you think it's significant?"

"Five-hundred-franc notes *are* on the conspicuous side. We want to draw as little attention to ourselves as possible. I'll have a word with the others when we meet at two o'clock. I'm going to the airport now to meet my wife off the lunchtime flight."

"I'll drive you, shall I?"

When Pauline came off the plane, she looked ravishing.

Blake drove us back to the hotel, and over lunch I told her how much money we had won. When she didn't seem particularly impressed I said, "You're not surprised we've done so well?"

"I'm only surprised you're still playing. I thought you would have been banned by now."

"Between you and me, I'm about as surprised as you are."

At the Massena I gave the group a general warning about the inadvisability of using 500-franc notes in restaurants and cafés. As the three musketeers were presumably still sleeping off the champagne they had consumed the night before I decided to save my warning against other forms of notoriety until later.

We arrived in the casino at the usual time of 2:45 P.M. As soon as play started three officials came to the table and tried to look over the shoulders of our six players. Mrs. Richardson immediately turned her notepad upside down. The others followed her example.

At 4:30 P.M. Maurice Nathan commenced a progression on *manque* (low). It went in fits and starts, not a steady predominance but protracted winning runs and then almost equally long adverse sequences when his line several times came down to two figures. It took him about an hour and a half to reach a stake above 2,000 francs. A hush fell on the crowd round the table, broken only by the clicking of the ivory ball and the calls of the croupiers.

The Chef de Casino came to the table. He had not smiled for several days.

At 5:45 P.M. Maurice Nathan looked up from his notepad and smiled. From the toppling piles of plaques and chips in front of him he carefully picked one pink 5-franc chip and placed it on *manque*. He had reached the table limit.

No casino official could be expected to see something like this without becoming hostile. We were making it all too obvious that not only could we win large sums (Nathan's mushroom brought him 40,300 francs—£2,900; $8,150), but that we would then deny them the chance to recover the money. This was a complete reversal of what is expected to happen between the player and the table (expected by the casino staff, of course—most players have the illusion they will win). Hunch gamblers will lose their fluky wins sooner or later and system players, if they are using an orthodox method, reach the table limit only when they are trying to recover previous losses, that is, when the table has been winning heavily.

On this occasion the quiet, almost mousy Maurice Nathan made it even more noticeable by the triumphant way he began to smile at everybody standing round the table, including the Chef de Casino. He had found in winning dramatically before a wide-eyed audience the chance to reveal the latent daredevil. Instead of shoving the larger denomination stuff into his pockets he left all his plaques and chips lying there in front of him.

For the first time in my obsessional affair with roulette I found myself praying that we would not have any more wins that day. The expressions of the Chef de Casino and his associates were alarming.

The inevitable happened. Of course. Almost as a punishment for my loss of nerve George Milton hit a progression on *passe*.

A man giving away gold bars in Trafalgar Square could not have drawn such a feverish audience. Eyes strained through tobacco smoke to see what he was writing in his notepad. Members of the staff appeared with notebooks of their own, each busily writing down every stake and result of Milton's progression.

As soon as Milton reached the table limit, crazy piles of rectangular plaques and round chips rising before him like the turrets of a gothic castle, I retreated to the bar.

No sooner was the whisky in my hand than two men approached me. Speaking in excellent English, one of them said, "Mr. Leigh?"

"Yes?"

"We understand you informed the Chef de Casino that you and your friends are a group formed to play roulette to a system."

"That is correct."

"We wonder, would you care to tell us something more about the system you are playing?"

"By all means." I pulled out my notebook and handed it to the one who was doing the talking. "If you'd like to write down your questions and sign the page at the bottom, I will be happy to answer anything you ask."

They frowned at each other, talked rapidly in French, shrugged and walked away.

Blake hurried towards me. "What did they want?" he asked.

"They wanted to interrogate me on our system. Strange, isn't it, how eager officials always are to ask questions and how reluctant to commit themselves on paper? I shouldn't panic."

"I'm worried," he said gravely.

The second shift played until 3 A.M. without another mushroom. All six players and myself were kept under

strict surveillance by the staff. When we left Blake was carrying 67,000 francs from the day's two progressions. Although we were well into October the temperature was still in the eighties and the combined effect of the heat and my customary twelve hours in the casino had made me too tired to find any great thrill in the sight of the money. Blake and I had 6,700 francs each (£490—$1,365) while the others had £355 ($994) apiece.

As soon as Blake had handed out the cash I stood up.

"It's very hot and we're all tired, so I'll be brief. The fact is that we are at the dangerous stage of this operation. You are finding that the novelty is wearing off—perhaps even the money is losing its thrill. We've had four successful days at the casino, and the management is clearly worried. Some of you may even think we've proved our point. Well, I haven't proved *my* point. To me this money is only the beginning. If we falter now, we'll be written off as a bunch of lucky amateurs who folded up before the real test. We can make gambling history, instead of just slipping off home with a few hundred pounds' profit. Of course we're getting heavy looks from the staff. Did you expect bouquets?"

"I don't know who could have been suggesting that we give up," Blake said sternly. "I'm certainly in no doubt that we should go on to the bitter end."

"Bitter end?" said Keith Robinson. "Seems pretty sweet to me." He held up his wad of francs. "I don't know what all the fuss is about. I've never had it so good. They can stare themselves blind at me for all I care. When they start whacking us over the skull with lead pipes that'll be the time to start moving."

"Of course we're going on," said Terry Baker quietly. "I'll work double shifts if anybody's thinking of walking out on us."

"Does everybody feel that way?" I asked. The eight

or nine present all nodded. "And do you agree that the team has a right to expect a hundred percent from each member? Yes. I'm glad of that because it makes the next thing I have to say easier. Quite apart from our winnings in the casino this whole town seems to be seething with gossip about wild parties—I've even heard them described as orgies. At the very least this is advertising our presence in the worst possible way. Now I'm not here to supervise morals. What I *am* concerned about is the risk of any one of us becoming known to the local police as an undesirable visitor. It's just the excuse they're looking for to throw us out of the country."

Careful as I had been not to look at anyone in particular, Alec Sherlock immediately assumed, rightly, that I was referring to him.

"There's no harm in a few bottles of champagne," he said.

"No harm at all if that's as far as it goes."

"Come along and see for yourself."

"I'm older than you. I need all the sleep I can get. I'm not mentioning anybody by name. What I am saying boils down to two points. One, the casino bars people who are suspected of association with criminals. Two, the group might have two or three days when it doesn't win anything. As we are all painfully aware, the Riviera is not the cheapest place in the world. I hope you are all putting enough to one side to see you through a lean spell."

"We haven't been spending all that much," said Sherlock. Terry Baker stared at his feet.

"A good deal more than you ever spent at home on champagne, I'd imagine," I said sharply. "Three hundred pounds in one night?"

"Yeah well, you're only young twice I always say," said Keith Robinson. "Don't worry—we've got a few bob tucked away under the mattress, haven't we?" He looked

at Sherlock and Terry Baker. They both nodded. "Rely on us, Norman," he said, getting up. "We'll be with you to the death. You two ready to blow?"

He said this to Baker and Sherlock. For a moment it looked as though Terry had decided to stay with the rest of us, but what chance did common sense have against the pull of a wild night with the boys, especially when his wife and child were due to arrive the next day?

As we were leaving his suite, Blake asked me to stay behind for a minute.

"I'm worried," he said.

"Oh, I was laying it on a bit thick. Baker's got a wife and child. The others can throw their money into the Mediterranean for all I care—"

"No, it's something else that's bothering me. Have you noticed that there's a pattern to the incidence of these progressions? I first spotted it in London. They generally seem to occur shortly after the same player has had one which petered out."

"I have noticed that. Almost like a warning, isn't it?"

"We've been having more than our fair share of these false starts in the last two days. I have the distinct feeling we're building up to a colossal bunching of limit reachers and table breakers."

"What's worrying about that?"

"The management is hostile enough as it is. I imagine they'd go berserk if we started having more progressions in a day."

"It's a risk we have to take," I said. "I'll walk home. Good night, Blake."

It was almost five when I got back to our room. Pauline woke up while I was undressing. "Emma said I was to tell you she spoke to her friend Philippe in the restaurant tonight," she said. "He came across to our table. She said

I wasn't to tell you in front of the others. He told her he knows all about her now. He said the whole town knows there's a successful team working in the municipal casino. She asked him if there was anything wrong in what you were doing and he said he could guarantee we wouldn't be doing it for much longer, but wouldn't say why."

"No, because he doesn't know himself. We won't be frightened off that easily."

As I climbed into bed she asked me, unable to control the worried note in her voice: "When does this stop, Norman?"

"It stops when we are stopped," I said firmly. Pauline accepted this and not once again in the fraught days that followed did she ever hint that she wanted me to give up.

The following day dawned hotter than ever—I say "dawned," but it was midday when I awoke. Pauline was already up. After breakfast we decided to take a stroll, ending up at Blake's hotel just after twelve. Blake's morning swim had cooled him off only temporarily. Incredibly he was back into his heavy blue suit. The heat was beginning to tell on his sixteen or seventeen stones. As we went out on the terrace of his hotel for a coffee he seemed to be moving with some effort, constantly touching his face with a large white handkerchief.

"I was followed this morning," he told us.

"I'm not unduly surprised," I said casually. "Round about now they're just beginning to think of ways to frighten us off. But we're not criminals and we're not robbing the casino: that's their problem. Nonetheless we're making serious inroads into the safe."

"I'm sure the same man has been watching me for a day or two," said Mrs. Harper-Biggs when I asked the first

shift if they had noticed anything. "I didn't like to say anything. Old women like me have a reputation for panicking unnecessarily."

"Why would they want to follow us?" asked Maurice Nathan.

"We are an unusual phenomenon, therefore we invite investigation," I said. "Don't worry about it. In fact, if you catch sight of the same man again, why not write down your name and address on a bit of paper and simply hand it to the man? Tell him it will save a lot of time and effort on his part if he simply comes along to see you at your hotel."

"That's a good idea," Mrs. Heppenstall commented calmly.

"Yes, I'd love to see the look on his face," said Mrs. Harper-Biggs.

It was on this day that Fredericks began to emerge from his shell. Although he was on the second shift he turned up that lunchtime at the Café Massena, so changed in appearance we didn't recognize him at first. He had been very busy that morning. He was wearing windscreen-shaped dark glasses, his mousy hair had been shampooed and restyled in a forwards direction to cover his thin patch —most startling of all, he had on a dove-grey silk suit that must have cost at least a couple of hundred pounds. He took our exclamations of surprise with undoubted pleasure. "I got a bit tired of looking like a dowdy office worker," he said.

"It looks very nice, Thomas," said Mrs. Richardson.

To go with his new image Fredericks went so far that particular lunchtime as to order not his usual ice-cream but a vermouth.

"Give him a couple of days and he'll be dashing off with the three musketeers for champagne orgies," said Milton.

"Has anybody seen a place that mends clothes in this town?" Maurice Nathan asked. He showed us a small tear in the pocket of his sports jacket. "Silly, really. I was in such a hurry to get here on time I barged against the door and caught the pocket on the handle."

"Round here they'll charge you the earth to mend it," said Mrs. Richardson. "Why don't you bring it round to my apartment when we finish this shift and I'll sew it up?"

"Oh no, this is your holiday. I wouldn't want to land you with housework—"

"If I don't have anything to do tonight I'll only end up watching another dreary French film in the fleapit."

"There is a cinema that shows English and American films," I said.

"Ah yes—we all went there the other night. What was that film called, Lettice?"

"*Guns Across the Rio Grande,*" Mrs. Heppenstall said authoritatively, adding with a trace of her old shy self, "I like cowboy films because it doesn't really matter who gets shot, does it?"

"I couldn't enjoy it for thinking how much it cost," said Mrs. Richardson. "Two pounds to see a bunch of cowboys? No thank you. No, Maurice, I insist. I can have that sewn up in three minutes."

This exchange, trivial in itself, may serve to illustrate how sensibly some of the party, especially the three ladies, took to the life of professional gambling. In fact, as I told Pauline that afternoon while we were watching play, I often thought I would have done better to recruit a team of women from the start. These three certainly showed more common sense than some of the men. Mrs. Harper-Biggs occasionally went up into the hills behind the town to looks for bugs and beetles. Mrs. Richardson's one indulgence was to have her hair done *every* morning. "It costs the *earth,*" she told Pauline, "but I don't suppose I'll ever

again have five pounds to throw away on one hairdo." Mrs. Heppenstall guiltily revealed that she was having regular manicures. They saved a few francs by going to a backstreet cinema which showed French films for the purely local audience; they organized such exotic escapades as supermarket explorations; Nathan hired a car and drove them to Monte Carlo for an early morning sightseeing trip. For two days or more we heard nothing else but descriptions of Prince Rainier's wonderful palace and of how they had actually seen Princess Grace, or someone remarkably like her.

"If I had twelve like them I think I would chance it and go for broke in the Salle Privée in Monte Carlo," I told Pauline one day. "I had a few words with Sherlock last night—but you can't tell a fool he's a fool, can you?"

One strange development was that Sherlock's complexion had cleared up remarkably in the few days we had been on the Riviera; a dull, respectable life in a London office is no match, it seems, for six hours gambling and champagne orgies till well after dawn when it comes to curing acne. The Riviera sun had nothing to do with it— I doubt if he saw the beach once during our whole stay.

The improvement in his skin, however, was not matched by a corresponding improvement in his character. He became much more confident but in an aggressive way. On one occasion when I was with him in the casino bar waiting for the shifts to change, I dropped him a hint about the advisability of saving some of the money he was making.

"You said we'd make a fortune and we're making it, so why the hell shouldn't we enjoy ourselves?" he said, annoyed.

"I never said we'd make a fortune," I corrected him. "But as we are doing well I'd like to see us all coming out of this with more money than when we started."

"Don't worry about me."

"I don't worry in the slightest about you. I don't care personally if you end up penniless. My only concern is to keep the team working smoothly."

"That's all right then," he said.

To Pauline I said, "We're on thin ice. You can't drink and fornicate every night without cracking up sooner or later."

"Maybe some of them need to go wild or they would explode," she suggested. "Look at poor Mr. Hopplewell."

"Poor? I should think he's one of the richest of the lot."

"I didn't mean that way. Do you know he drinks two bottles of brandy a day? He told me the other night when we went to eat in that bistro by the Quay."

"I knew he liked his brandy—but two bottles a day!"

"He's an alcoholic. He told me all about it. He can't do without it, so apparently he goes through sheer torture playing for six hours with only one or two. That's why he wanted to go on the early shift—to avoid the temptation of going back to Blake's suite for the share-outs. He thinks you're all watching him. So he just goes to his own room with a bottle and quietly drinks the lot. He doesn't drink to get drunk, but just so that he can feel normal. He's a very nice man, actually, if you can get him talking. His children won't have anything to do with him because of his drinking. Do you know he has five grandchildren he's never been allowed to see? Isn't that cruel?"

"I've had dealings with alcoholics, darling. He probably put his family through unmitigated hell. Pity we're not working twelve-hour shifts; in time he might be cured altogether."

"They're not machines, you know. Honestly, Norman, your attitude is very brutal."

"I don't have time to be a father confessor. If the money brings out the hidden truth about their real characters, I'm not to blame, am I?"

"No, but you could be more sympathetic."

"Making people rich is sympathetic enough as far as I'm concerned."

This conversation did make me think. As we crossed the sun-scorched square towards the casino on our fifth day, Mrs. Harper-Biggs and Mrs. Heppenstall on either side of Emma Richardson, Maurice Nathan discussing French cars with Milton, Hopplewell and myself in the rear, they all seemed like different people. Yet, at the same time, I had a strange feeling that I had known them all my life. I realized it mattered to me that *they* came out of this with —well, with money, certainly, but something more besides. In my obsession with proving that I could beat the casino I had had to ignore them as individuals, to relegate them to the role of puppets whose purpose was to make my plan succeed. I suppose I was actually finding a belated sense of humanity. At the time I told myself I was merely grateful to them for not having let me down.

Day five. The casino made another move against us. When we got to our table all the seats had already been taken, though it was only 2:50 p.m. The people occupying the chairs looked like ordinary players. Obviously I couldn't ask them if they had been prompted to grab the seats by the management. It seemed too much of a coincidence, however.

"Just stand as close to the chairs as possible and grab them as they become vacant," I instructed the first shift. "If you get into any difficulty let me know. I'll take over and give you a rest."

Having seen them place their first pink 5-franc chips, I said to Pauline that we should lose ourselves in the throngs of the large salon.

"They know the system backwards now," I said, "and

standing is sheer torture. Keep an eye on Mrs. Harper-Biggs in case she looks like fainting."

Standing within viewing distance of our table some ten minutes later, I saw Milton signalling to me. I went across.

"They seem to have stopped the waiters from serving us," he said, leaning forward to place the chips for his next bet on *passe* (high). "I asked that old bugger for a coffee ten minutes ago. He's been back with drinks for other people but not for me."

"I'll have a word with him."

I went across to the oldest of the waiters, a man whose face told of unspeakable anguish and suffering. ("It's their feet, poor devils," Blake said.)

"I'd like a coffee for my friend," I said politely, pointing to Milton. The old idiot shrugged and walked away.

"Only a cup of coffee, but in these circles a sure sign that war has been officially declared," I said to Pauline.

It didn't take long for hostilities to be stepped up.

· 13

The casino's next move was more subtle.

The first shift had been playing for an hour and a half when Mrs. Harper-Biggs simultaneously got a seat and started a progression on her chance, *impair* (the odd numbers). After nine spins her line read something like 3, 4, 7, 10, 13, 16 and her next stake was 19 francs, nothing to excite any casual observer. However, four or five women standing at her corner of the table began to ask her questions, the usual things people ask at a roulette table: What number came up last? What colour is predominating? What system are you using?

These women were of differing ages, fairly well dressed but nothing out of the ordinary. Until then there had been nothing to suggest that they were together.

As I moved nearer, Mrs. Harper-Biggs was on spin 14, and her line read 7, 10, 13, 17. She won 24 francs and added that figure to the end of her line, giving her a stake for spin 15 of 7 + 24—31. This lost. On spin 16 her stake was 10 + 17—27. This won. Only 27 francs, but the women round her increased the intensity of their questions, speaking rapidly in French. I knew then they were no ordinary players but an organized group deliberately setting out to upset her concentration.

Mrs. Harper-Biggs did not need me to tell her to ignore them. They began to ask the same questions in English. Mrs. Harper-Biggs went on ignoring them, only a tightening of her mouth indicating that she was conscious of their presence. By spin 23 her line read 17, 27, 37, 54 giving her a stake of 71 francs. She lost, bringing her line down to two figures, 27, 37. Then she had four wins in a row. By spin 27 her line was 27, 37, 64, 91, 118, giving her a stake of 145 francs. The women tried to put her off by pushing even closer, firing questions from all sides, even going so far as to nudge her elbow. At this she looked up and gave the offending female a glare of the kind that had no doubt kept the late Mr. Harper-Biggs in line.

I eased myself between the woman on her left hand and the chair to lend her moral support.

By spin 33 her line read 37, 64, 91, 118, 155, 192, 229, 266. This looked very promising, with enough of the lower figures left to give her a chance of progressing slowly to the limit and thereby having more winning bets on the way than would have been the case if wins and losses had alternated in such a way as to delete the smaller figures early in the sequence.

During all this these determined she-wolves kept yapping at her from all sides. A hardened professional gambler would have found it hard to maintain concentration, but for her, a rather grand lady of uncertain temperament, to keep on with her calculations and find the exact plaques and chips for each stake was a tremendous feat of concentration. I was proud of her.

It was a long and profitable ordeal. It took her over two hours to reach the table limit. By that time, however, the team of women had decided she could not be upset and had turned their attentions on Mrs. Richardson, who had started a small progression on her chance, red. I had no doubt then that they were working under instructions

to concentrate on flustering whichever of our players was having a winning sequence.

They started asking Mrs. Richardson the same questions. Mrs. Richardson ignored them. Meanwhile the croupiers were sending out the usual alert by handclap, and a fair crowd was assembling at the table.

One of the women leaned over and started fiddling with Mrs. Richardson's chips.

"I'll help you put them in order," she said in French. Mrs. Richardson calmly pushed her arm away. I eased over and stood by her.

"It's all right," said Mrs. Richardson grimly.

"Don't give them the satisfaction of upsetting you," I said, arranging her chips and plaques in some semblance of order. Red was predominating in fits and starts, and at several stages her line was down to two figures, but always it took life again.

Mrs. Harper-Biggs reached the limit at about twenty minutes to seven. Her progression had lasted over two hours. Mrs. Richardson reached the limit about half an hour later, although hers had lasted less than two hours. (This may sound like an account of unbroken triumph, but during this time the other four members of the shift were losing steadily on short sequences.) There were two winning progressions on that shift of six hours at thirty spins to the hour. As a collective unit our six players made over a thousand separate bets in that shift. To get the two winning progressions Mrs. Harper-Biggs and Mrs. Richardson possibly had fewer than two hundred winning bets between them.

As Mrs. Richardson pulled the scattered piles of plaques and chips together the Chef de Casino came close to the table and glowered at her.

Mrs. Richardson gave him a sweet smile and started

betting again—one miserable 5-franc chip. The Chef muttered something and stalked off.

The rest of that day passed without incident, excepting the blanket refusal to serve any of us with coffee or drinks, a small argument over seats when the shifts changed and a noticeable slowness on the part of the croupiers when any of our team asked them to change a high-denomination plaque into smaller chips.

There were no more progressions. The first shift went off to eat, but several of them returned later in the evening. Only Mrs. Heppenstall, Mrs. Harper-Biggs and Hopplewell were missing when we met in Blake's hotel for the share-out. Everybody was complaining about the strain of having to stand and go without refreshment.

"I don't mind telling you I was near to screaming when those women kept pestering me," said Mrs. Richardson.

"They gave up in the end," I said. "I thought you and Mrs. H-B did extraordinarily well. If that's the best they can do we've got them beaten."

"Was I seeing things, or did anybody else notice lights flashing?" Fredericks asked.

"I saw something flashing, too," said Maurice Nathan. "I thought it was bulbs burning out in the chandeliers."

"No, it was a flash camera," said Sherlock. "I saw the bloke taking pictures."

Nobody else had seen a photographer, it seemed.

"Who knows, in a few weeks you may see photographs of yourselves as part of the international jet-set elite," I said. "How did we do, anyway, Mr. Blake?"

"Not bad, considering the difficulties we were under. Two progressions—a healthy figure of fifty-five thousand three hundred and eighty-five francs."

"Can't be bad," said Keith Robinson, rubbing his hands together. Terry Baker thought otherwise.

"I don't think it's all that brilliant," he complained. "We're getting a lot of abortive runs petering out halfway. I still think we would save a lot of time by going for the high stakes in the Monte Carlo casino rather than carrying on here day after day for dribs and drabs."

"I daresay three or four hundred pounds a day hardly meets your bar bill," Blake said icily.

There was an embarrassed pause. Baker blushed and for a few seconds it seemed that he might bluster. Then, calmly, he said, "All right. No point in denying it. I've been chucking money away like a drunken sailor. Still, my wife's arriving tomorrow, so the party's over. From now on I'll behave."

Blake did the sharing out. He and I had 5,538 francs each, about £400 ($1,120). The other eleven shared 44,309 francs, giving them about 4,028 francs each, about £294 ($822). Everyone departed.

Baker brought his wife and baby from the airport in time for the usual rendezvous at the Café Massena the next day, our sixth day at the Casino Municipale. Lyn Baker was a quiet little girl with a pale face, hardly into her twenties. It looked as though they had already been arguing in the taxi, for he was looking very grim. I had been hoping for an extrovert wife with a temperament robust enough to put the reins on Terry, but the more I watched her listening nervously to what must have been our incomprehensible discussion about casino tactics the more I felt certain her presence might even make the situation worse.

On our way across the square to the casino I held Pauline back. Terry and his wife were still sitting outside the café.

"If you get a chance to speak to her alone, do you think you could persuade her to go straight back home?" I said.

"I'll suggest it to Terry, but you know how obstinate he can be."

"It might calm him down a bit having her here with the baby."

"More likely it will be too much for his emotional capacity to cope with. They're all complaining already about the strain we're under—how's he going to react with her and the baby hanging about all the time?"

"But you said having her here would stop him throwing his money away! You don't mind if he's broke as long as he keeps playing, is that it?"

It was a question I couldn't answer.

When we entered the salon at 2:50 P.M. only two of the chairs at our table were occupied. Milton and Nathan elected to stand. I saw no signs of the women who had tried to harass Mrs. Richardson and Mrs. Harper-Biggs the day before. The table staff were, as always, bland and polite.

At 3:30 P.M. Nathan hit a progression on *manque* (low —numbers one to eighteen). Within twenty spins he was staking 100 francs (about £7, or $20). The handclapping started. Senior members of the staff arrived at the table to have huddled conversations with each other. Another ten spins took Nathan to a stake of 500 francs. The Chef de Casino came to the table. Nathan had a phenomenal run of consecutive wins, the ball dropping in low numbers eight successive times. His lowest number on the line was 135, which meant that his stakes increased by only 135 units at each spin, giving him a satisfyingly long line of winning bets. When he reached the table limit he had won 27,475 francs (approximately £2,000–$5,600). In total silence he put the large plaques into his pockets.

He smiled graciously as bystanders tried to question

him about his system. The Chef de Casino kept remarkable control of himself. Only the fists clenched at the seams of his trousers showed the extent of his anger. When one of the spectators made a joke to him about the Englishman bankrupting the casino he even managed a tight-lipped smile.

Blake arrived in the salon a few minutes later. He listened impassively as I told him about Nathan's progression.

"Our good friend Monsieur le Chef looked fit to go out of his mind," I said. "I think we can expect fresh countermeasures."

"To hell with him," Blake said grimly. "They're so damn used to fleecing tourists they can't tolerate anybody who gives them a run for their money. If they want to cause trouble we'll give them a fight."

From a man whose punctilious avoidance of any form of unpleasantness marked him out from the rest, this new attitude was surprising.

Around 6:30 P.M. George Milton started on a progression of the very best kind, from our point of view. The predominance of *passe* (high—numbers nineteen to thirty-six) made itself felt when his line still comprised low numbers, something like 42, 56, 73. Normally a predominance averages 5 to 2 or even 3 to 1 over its opposite, but this doesn't mean that the player has five wins followed by two losses and so on. More likely the arbitrary patterns thrown up by the wheel (detectable only as patterns in retrospect) would give freak runs of seven, eight or nine consecutive wins followed by one loss and then another five wins.

Milton's progression went on so long that soon every senior member of the casino staff was watching him.

They had the galling experience of witnessing a table breaker. As our pubkeeper stalwart was about to place

a stake well below the table maximum, around 2,000 francs, the Chef de Partie announced that play was temporarily suspended at that table. It had run out of plaques!

"It's their own fault. They've been hoist by their own damned cleverness," I said to Blake.

"How is that?" He seemed preoccupied.

"They were paying Milton in high-denomination stuff, five-hundred-franc plaques, even a thousand-franc plaque, then they were taking their time about giving him change, hoping he couldn't get the proper stake together before 'Rien ne va plus.' Now they've run out of the big stuff."

Milton sat there wiping his forehead while the crowd stood silently watching him.

"I think I'll have a drink," I muttered to Blake. "It's getting a bit hot in here."

I had hardly finished my whisky when Blake came hurrying into the bar. "I think you should come back to the table," he said urgently. "Mrs. Heppenstall is on to something."

This was probably the moment that made up the minds of the casino bigwigs to take conclusive action against us. Milton had just won 32,000 francs on a progression where high had predominated for almost two hours. No sooner had play recommenced at our table than the wheel began to throw up a predominance of *pair* (even) over *impair* (odd).

No matter which way the wheel went, it was now startlingly obvious, it was bound to favour us. Milton was back to bets of a few meaningless francs, while Mrs. Heppenstall was busily reaping the profits from the wheel's change of mood.

Whether the crowds who gathered round the table to watch the little Englishwoman in the plain summer dress scooping in the chips understood any of this is hard to say; they certainly sensed that something unnatural was

happening. So many people crowded forward to watch that the waiters had to ask them to move away so that they could serve the òther players—not, of course, our players. The heat and the smoke became unbearable.

"How she's coping I'm damned if I know," said Blake. "I could quite easily faint just standing here watching."

"There's nothing we can do. Let's go and have a drink."

The barman took ten minutes to serve us, although he was by no means busy. We looked through the open doorway to the roulette tables. Our table was surrounded by at least a hundred people all pushing forward, none too decorously, to get a view of this famous syndicate in action.

"I wonder how many of them are desperately rushing to get bets on *pair* just because Lettice is betting on it," I said to Blake.

"They were doing that when Hopplewell had a tiny little progression—they certainly seem to know every one of us by sight now."

"Might be better if Lettice doesn't reach the limit then. If even half a dozen people follow her all the way, the casino will be cleaned out."

"Wasn't that part of your idea?"

"What, to break the bank altogether? Not at all."

"I had the distinct impression you wanted to bring this place to its knees."

"It would certainly be a coup, but let's be practical: killing the golden goose and all that . . ."

"To hell with them, I say. If we break this place we can always go to another." He spoke with a bitterness I had not heard in his voice before. Pauline came out of the crowd and hurried towards us. She was just telling us that Mrs. Heppenstall had reached the limit (she had

won 11,768 francs) when Peter Vincent ambled into the bar.

"Hello, you chaps," he drawled. "How are things at the cash and carry?"

Blake looked at his watch. "Ten to nine," he snapped. "Time we were getting in position for the seats." He left abruptly.

"Glass of wine I fancy," said Vincent, in near-perfect imitation of Blake's voice. He caught my eye and smiled. "Pity you're stuck in here all day, Mr. Leigh. Wonderful swimming down here."

The bar staff were continuing to ignore us, and he was unable to get service. I went with him to the table to see the shifts change. Three failed to get seats, one of them being Blake, whose weight must have heightened his general discomfort as the crowds—and the heat—increased.

Paradoxically, the team's fame began to help us here. Having become celebrities, every bet made by the team was watched and copied by dozens of other players. This meant that Blake was given ample elbow room to place his stakes, though he still had to do his calculations with the notepad balanced on his forearm and his hand full of plaques.

Fredericks, who was also standing, hit a progression on black just before midnight. It turned out to be one of the most protracted mushrooms we had experienced. After eighteen spins the lowest number on his line was still 6. After an hour the poor man was almost in a state of collapse. I stood beside him and eventually took over his paperwork. The progression lasted for two and a quarter hours. By the time the line was producing stakes of 2,000 francs Fredericks was only going through the motions. I was doing the paperwork, telling him what

plaques and chips he needed for his next stake, finally even placing the stakes for him, leaving him the minor task of picking up our winnings. His brilliant new suit began to bulge with the chips we were winning.

We reached the limit around 2:30 A.M.

Never was 1, 2, 3, 4 written on a clean page with such relief. It was a colossal mushroom considering that it had not broken the table—no less than 51,760 francs.

There wasn't much of a turnout at Blake's place that morning. Fredericks went to his hotel, saying that if he had only one drink his legs would fall off. The novelty of seeing bundles of francs being counted out had worn off. None of the first shift had bothered to return to the casino after dinner.

"Not a bad day," said Blake when he looked up from his cash book. "From four progressions we made exactly one hundred and twenty-three thousand and three francs. Satisfactory, Mr. Leigh?"

"How do we share out the three spare francs?" asked Keith Robinson. Nobody else found this funny at the time, but it made me laugh uncontrollably. Maybe it was a delayed reaction to the tension of the evening. The rest of them waited until I was able to regain my composure.

"I'm sorry," I said. "Let's leave the three francs as a floating cash reserve."

That started Keith off. Watching him heave with laughter, I seemed to see another man altogether, a much stronger and resourceful character than the quasi-cockney joker. He has had the right attitude towards all this, I thought: win, spend it, keep a smile on your face. He would survive, no matter what.

Blake announced the results of his arithmetic. He and I had 12,300 francs each, not far short of £900 ($2,490). The other eleven shared 98,400, a share each of 8,945

francs, £652 ($1,825). He handed out the cash to those present: Sherlock, Robinson, Baker, Vincent and myself.

"I think I should drive you home, Mr. Leigh," suggested Blake.

Outside, Keith Robinson made some remark about the town's night life only starting at dawn. Terry Baker hesitated.

"Come on," said Keith. "The morning's only young yet."

"Aren't you going back to your wife and child?" Blake said.

"Why the hell should I?" asked Baker. "I've got the rest of my life to go home early, haven't I?"

He went off with Robinson and Sherlock. Vincent stretched his arms and yawned. "Nice night for a swim, eh?" he said. Incredibly he started into a little tap dance, singing, "I like swimmin' with wimmin, and wimmin like swimmin' with me." Blake stared at him. Vincent gave us a deep bow, ambled off to his car and had soon roared off in it.

"The man's unbalanced," Blake said as we got into his car.

"I think he knows what he's doing," I said. "Baker's the one who is genuinely unbalanced. Would you like to guess how much of that money sees daylight?"

"I daresay the strain is beginning to tell."

"If they drank less and got more sleep, they wouldn't find it such a strain."

"On their own heads be it."

"I think it's *pitiful*. Hundreds of tax-free pounds a day —and they decide to chuck it away as fast as they get their hands on it. Do they think we'll be allowed to go on winning forever? Bloody fools. And Baker with that child-wife of his! I'd like to shake him until—"

"As you said, this isn't a Boy Scout troop. You've shown them how to make money. You can't be expected to wet-nurse them through life as well."

"I must be going soft."

As he dropped me at my hotel he suggested we should pray for cooler weather. It was not until I was in bed that I realized why our conversation had felt so strange. He had been saying the things I should have been saying. I lay there in the dark, too tired to sleep, listening to the endless chirruping of the accursed cicadas.

Day seven. Another scorcher. Baker's wife turned up at the Café Massena with their child but without Baker. She said he was still in bed. Pauline had told me that morning that Lyn Baker was more mature than one might have guessed: "She's had a lot of trouble with Terry," she said. "She didn't tell us in so many words, but I think he didn't leave the police solely to come on this trip. More likely he jumped before he was pushed. She can't get him to save any of the money!"

"Married too young I suppose—same old story."

"She says she's hoping he'll get rid of all his bad blood on this trip and then be prepared to settle down."

"I should say she's being wildly optimistic."

We crossed the square at 2:45 P.M. As we went in out of the sunshine I realized that I was almost wishing the whole thing was over. Six hours' sleep had not been enough. The six members of the first shift, Emma, Lettice Heppenstall, Mrs. Harper-Biggs, Sydney Hopplewell, Maurice Nathan and George Milton, all looked fresh and unworried—but they had finished at 9 P.M. the previous night and gone off to dinner and an early bed. I had eaten breakfast and lunch within an hour of each other,

had a bath, put on clean clothes and come straight to the Massena with Pauline.

As soon as we left the relentless glare of the street for the shabby gloom of the casino entrance, we were once again in the timeless, unreal world of the gaming salon, our existences governed by a segmented wheel, an ivory ball, a numbered grid of green baize. Even the six people I knew had the remoteness of strangers, as if they might be half-remembered faces from a dream. Had *I* brought that imposing woman in the green tweed suit to a foreign country to take part in this monotonous ritual?

Past and future do not exist in the casino. We had all become part of an endless charade. Practical motives had long been forgotten—we were here simply because we were here. It had been ordained.

But six days in the Casino Municipale had made considerable inroads on my reserves of stamina and will-power. I was near delirium.

14

At 3:35 P.M. on that scorching afternoon Mrs. Harper-Biggs ran into a progression on *impair* (odd numbers). Within twenty minutes the table was surrounded. The usual handclapping, which we were all beginning to find less ominous than boring, brought the distraught Chef de Casino to our table. In something like forty spins Mrs. Harper-Biggs' stakes were hovering under the limit of 2,600 francs.

Then she ran into an adverse sequence where the ball favoured the even numbers. Just as quickly as the chips had accumulated they began to dwindle, each even number demolishing more and more of her line. Eventually she had only three figures left. Two more losses would have wiped her out on that sequence. The Chef de Casino looked pleased: perhaps our system was going to fail like all the others.

Then Mrs. Harper-Biggs found that the wheel was favouring her again. To everybody's amazement she reached the limit at 5:30, winning 15,645 francs. I made a point of not catching the eye of my old friend M. le Chef.

To take some of the work off her hands I arranged her plaques and chips into some kind of order while she

reverted to 1, 2, 3, 4 and placed a pink chip on *impair*. The silence of the crowd round the table was eerie, broken only by the buzzing of wasps or flies.

Mrs. Harper-Biggs won her first bet on the new sequence. She staked 6 francs. *Impair* paid off again.

Within twenty minutes she had hit *another* progression!

The faces of the Chef de Casino, the Chef de Partie and their minions were varied in reaction from astonishment to downright chagrin. This was impossible—but it was happening, here and now, every assumption of their professional lives being proved wrong. No longer could the English team's system be written off as a fluke. For six days we had laboured profitably and now on the seventh we were reaping a golden harvest. The rules which governed the closed world of the casino had been completely reversed. Even the croupiers, who until then had maintained a neutral attitude to our successes, were visibly impressed.

At 6:45 P.M. Mrs. Harper-Biggs reached the table limit for the second time and once again wrote 1, 2, 3, 4 on a clean page. I do not believe there was a single player at any of the other tables.

"Would you like me to take your place for a while?" I said, controlling an urge to pat her on her tweedy back.

"I would," she said flatly. I slipped into her chair before anyone knew she was getting up.

Nothing much happened to the six of us until around 8 P.M. when I commenced a small progression on *impair*. It looked like petering out on several occasions but then picked up in no uncertain fashion. Soon I was staking 1,000 francs and more.

For the first time I began to experience the incredible tension of being the center of attraction. As I struggled with the flow of chips and the unwieldy figures I was

having to add I felt inadequate. I was as nervous as a beginner. The handclapping began to sound threatening. Whenever I looked up from my notepad to place a stake I could see only those eyes staring at me, scores of them, women's eyes, old men's eyes, hostile eyes, jealous eyes, lascivious eyes, all of them on me.

The progression lasted until just before 9 P.M. Almost breathless from the heat and lack of oxygen, I did a quick calculation, assembled a handful of high-denomination plaques and some chips, pushed them forward to the rectangle marked *impair*—and saw a hand restraining my wrist.

Looking up, I found the croupier shaking his head at me.

The stake I had tried to put was 2,750 francs—150 francs above the limit.

I sat back, blinking stupidly at the vast spew of plastic in front of me. The eyes. Silence.

One face stood out from the rows around and above me, that of the Chef de Casino.

As I wrote 1, 2, 3, 4 on the fresh page I could not help sneaking looks at him. His solid, shiny face was like stone.

I leaned forward with my first pink 5-franc chip. Suddenly it all seemed too much. I had won all this and I was betting a pathetic 5 francs?

I laughed out loud.

The Chef de Casino's face contorted with fury. Pointing to me, he shook one of his assistants by the arm. "*C'est le chef* [He's the boss]," he barked, and strode off.

Some of the people nearest me patted my back, loudly congratulating me on this achievement. I said nothing, bitterly regretting the momentary loss of control that had made me laugh out loud. To the Chef de Casino it must have been an unforgivable insult.

The second shift took over at 9 P.M. Blake offered no

explanation as to why he had turned up only in time to take his place at the table. I went with George Milton and Emma to the bar. We were all shaken.

"Three progressions on one shift—all on the same chance?" said Milton, his solid ex-sergeant's face aghast.

"I don't know why we're so nervy," said Emma, giggling. "This is what we came for. We're going to be rich. Come on, Norman, relax—"

"We're killing the goose," I said. "Two progressions a day and they might have tolerated us for a while longer, but three—besides, I tried to stake above the limit. I could kick myself."

"Yes, well, you haven't had the practice we've had," George said sympathetically. The three of us found this very funny. Pauline couldn't understand what we were laughing at when she came to pick up Emma for dinner. I had a quick snack in the casino restaurant and went back to the table.

Madness continued to reign that day.

Peter Vincent got a progression on *manque* (low), within forty minutes of sitting down. It was a monster! It took him until 11 P.M. to reach the limit, one of the largest mushrooms of all (48,640 francs at the count), an amazing amount to have won without breaking the table.

While he was handling this monstrous sequence Fredericks got a progression on black. He went very quickly to the limit, finishing long before Peter and winning a mere 12,895 francs—£940 ($2,610).

It dawned on me as Vincent came to the end of his mushroom that something was missing. There had been no handclapping. And the Chef de Casino had not appeared.

"Even he's got to sleep sometime," Emma said when she and Pauline, Maurice and George came back to the casino at midnight.

Coming back from the bar, I noticed something else.

Standing in a group at one end of the table were a group of odd-looking men—odd in the sense that they were dressed more appropriately for a merchant bank than a casino on the Côte d'Azur, formal lounge suits and stiff collars. They looked at me in a manner which suggested they knew all about me and wanted only to check my appearance.

At 2 A.M. Fredericks got another progression on black, one we could well have done without.

Two of these men in the lounge suits moved round the table to stand behind his chair. Without any attempt at concealment they peered over his shoulder to see what he was writing in his notepad.

I signalled to him from the other side of the table and he immediately cradled the pad with his left arm.

When he reached the limit it was five minutes to three. The casino was nearly empty apart from the curious hard core at our table.

"Don't bother starting again," I said to Fredericks, signalling to the other five to leave the table. He had won 26,500 francs on his second progression. We had to help Blake cash up at the desk. Never before had I seen so many plaques and chips being exchanged for cash.

It took Blake half an hour to count out the piles of francs on his Georgian dining table. Most of us just sat there and stared, too tired or too astounded to shout for joy. "One hundred and fifty-nine thousand six hundred and sixty francs," Blake said eventually, with a note of awe in his voice.

The money was shared out. Blake and I had about £1,150 each (about $3,220). The eleven others got a fraction less than £850 ($2,380) each.

"You know, I think we've only just started," Blake said. "Can't you feel it in your bones? Didn't I tell you this would happen, Mr. Leigh?"

Keith Robinson and Sherlock were already on their feet.

"I shouldn't allow yourselves to be carried away by today's events," I said coldly. "This bunching of progressions can do us nothing but harm. Six mushrooms in one day will be intolerable as far as the casino is concerned. There were some strange faces watching us tonight. We will have to be even more careful about everything we do in the casino. Mrs. Harper-Biggs was near to fainting today. If you think you're going to faint, let me know immediately. If I'm not available and you're going to pass out, make a note on your pad of what your next stake would have been and leave the table. Start where you left off when you next take up play."

"You don't think maybe we should move to another casino?" Sherlock said. "Give this place a chance to cool off?"

"Why move?" George Milton retorted. "They haven't thrown us out yet, have they? I'm buggered if I'm going to start trekking up and down the south of bloody France like a gypsy—I like it here."

"We wouldn't gain anything by moving," I said. "Every municipal casino will have heard of us by now. Anything planned for us here would happen just as quickly anywhere else. We'll carry on as we're doing and let the casino make the first move. Now if you'll excuse me I must get some sleep."

October 7 dawned just as hot as before, but when we opened the windows there was a slight breeze blowing off the Mediterranean.

"Thank God for that," I said to Pauline. "Let's pray it whips up a gale through that casino."

Over breakfast I told her about the money we had won the day before. "Almost twelve hundred pounds for

us, in one day—not such a hare-brained scheme after all, was it?"

"What will the casino do now?"

"That's the interesting part."

"Funnily enough I don't think you would really be sorry if they stopped you."

"Whatever gave you that idea?"

When we met at the Massena at 2 P.M. most of the group were looking apprehensive.

"I'm surprised at you all," I said briskly. "I thought you'd be enthusing just a little over the money we won yesterday."

"It doesn't seem like real money actually," said Mrs. Harper-Biggs. "It comes too easily, I suppose."

"It's funny," said George Milton. "If you'd told me a few months ago I could be knocking down five or six hundred quid a day for a few hours' roulette I'd have been like a cat on hot bricks, but after a while it gets monotonous, doesn't it?"

"It's what most people fail to understand about being wealthy," Blake drawled. "Why doesn't the millionaire stop working, sort of thing. As Mr. Leigh told us months ago, most people are much happier losing—they wouldn't admit it, of course."

"As a matter of fact I think Norman was wrong there," George said quietly but with enough authority to let Blake know he was not to be patronized. "Most people only put up with losing because nobody's ever told them how to win."

"Most people are pretty lazy," said Mrs. Harper-Biggs. Lettice Heppenstall shook her head.

"I couldn't disagree more, Cynthia," she said. "I think most people are much better than everyone gives them credit for."

Although they had seemingly become close friends it was not the first time in the last two or three days I had noticed Mrs. Heppenstall turning quite sharply on Mrs. Harper-Biggs. The flustered, self-effacing little widow had acquired a lot of new confidence in herself, perhaps in the knowledge that she was just as important to the team as anyone else. They were all changing in some way or another. George Milton had such a tan he was beginning to look positively Italian. Maurice Nathan, who had been almost primly reserved when I first met him, now stared openly at the legs of any woman who passed in front of the café and was becoming quite sharp with the waiters.

We crossed the square at 2.45 P.M. In the salon there was no sign of the men in regulation suits.

"Seems a lot cooler," said Pauline.

"You're the only one who's never complained about the heat, love," George Milton said to Mrs. Heppenstall, patting her on the back. "You'd do well in a pub, actually. You should think of that with all this gelt you're tucking away."

"Lettice in a *pub*?" said Mrs. Harper-Biggs severely. "Ridiculous."

"I haven't been in a pub since the end of the war," Mrs. Heppenstall said calmly. "I must come and visit yours, George."

"Drinks on the house, Lettice," he said, giving her a thumbs-up. Mrs. Harper-Biggs grimaced.

At 3:30 the fun started. Two progressions occurred simultaneously, Maurice Nathan on *manque* (low), Sydney Hopplewell on black.

"The fat's in the fire now," I said to Pauline. The handclaps started while both of them were still staking under the 100-franc mark. The Chef de Casino came to the table for his customary inspection of the people who

were eating into his profits. When our eyes met I was struck by the change in his manner. The man seemed positively serene!

Maurice and Sydney both had short progressions which jointly netted a mere 37,000 francs.

They had barely restarted with 1, 2, 3, 4 when six men wearing suits of a cut and quality rarely seen in France came into the salon.

"That's officialdom of a very high order or I'm much mistaken," Blake said.

The six men broke up as they came to our table, and each took up position directly behind one of our first shift. They brought out notebooks and started to copy what our players were writing in their notepads. I signalled to the six to hide their figures, but the six officials merely waited until the stakes were placed before entering the amounts in their books.

"They're going to write down every stake and every result for this session," Blake said. "That should more or less give them everything they need to know about our system, damn them."

"But they must know by now what system you're using," Pauline said.

"The Chef de Casino knows, but these chaps are from higher up," I told her. "Ministry of the Interior probably. Flattering, isn't it?"

"I don't like the sound of that," said Blake.

Mrs. Harper-Biggs—or rather the wheel—could not have chosen a worse time to commence a progression on *impair* (odd).

"They'll get the whole picture now," I said, watching the spy behind Mrs. Harper-Biggs carefully noting everything she did.

"Why don't we call everybody off for the day, Mr.

Leigh?" Black suggested. "That would spike their guns."

"No, they'll come back tomorrow and the day after if needs be. We might as well push the damn thing to the limit now."

Mrs. Harper-Biggs' progression petered out. For half an hour our six players did nothing more dramatic than lose a series of 10 francs.

At 7:30 P.M. the six mystery men put away their notebooks and left the table.

"They've tumbled the system or else they've got writer's cramp," I said.

"Don't sound so cheerful about it," said Blake.

"I like a bit of drama—proves we're hitting them hard, doesn't it?"

"I don't want drama. I want to go on winning money."

During the next twenty minutes Sydney Hopplewell got a start on black. It took him until well after nine to reach the limit, having won 18,390 francs. When Thomas Fredericks took over his chair at the end of the progression he said, as he passed us: "If I don't get a drink, I'll fall apart."

"Well, well," I said to Pauline, "you realize he just went six and a half hours without one single brandy?"

"I don't think the temperance movement would be too keen on gambling as a cure for drinking."

Midnight. Keith Robinson started on a two-hour progression. The Chef de Casino arrived at the table in response to the handclapping. Keith was on a beauty, his stakes going up by only around 50 francs or so at a time, this slow progress to the limit giving him what seemed like a yard of uncrossed figures on his line, all of them representing winning bets.

While he was raking in the chips in veritable piles Alec Sherlock got a progression on *pair* (even). Keith reached

the limit after something like sixty-six spins. He had won no less than 47,665 francs. Sherlock's stakes went up to the 1,000-franc mark.

A waiter came across the salon and handed a note to the Chef de Casino. He read it and then walked quickly to the exit. It was 2:15 A.M. Sherlock reached the limit at 2:25 A.M. He had won a lot less than Keith, 16,540 francs. I told the team to pack it in for the day.

As we cashed in our masses of plaques and chips the Chef de Casino stood a few feet away, watching us impassively.

Back in Blake's suite we shared out 119,595 francs. Blake and I split 23,919 francs and the remaining 95,676 divided eleven ways gave each of the team about 8,700 francs each, about £630 ($1,775). As Vincent said, picking up his bundle of 100- and 500-franc notes, "All this paper is beginning to clutter up my pockets."

"Come and spend some of it with us," said Keith Robinson. Vincent shook his head.

"Where do you go when you're not playing?" Sherlock demanded. Vincent turned on him and said, in his most insulting drawl, "I got over the thrill of having *two* prostitutes at a time some time ago."

"What the hell do you mean by that?" Sherlock snapped.

"Let's not have any unpleasantness," Blake said firmly. "We're all very tired and may say stupid things we'll regret in the clear light of day. I suggest we all plod off to our respective digs."

"I don't want to sound defeatist," Fredericks said, "but I don't think Mrs. Harper-Biggs is going to last out much longer. The atmosphere in there is unbearable."

"Mrs. Harper-Biggs will last as long as any of us," I said. "I would hope that none of you was so naive as to believe it would be a cakewalk to take this amount of

money from a casino. Of course they have been trying to intimidate us and of course it would be very cosy if we just packed it in now and went home. But I didn't come all this way to give up as soon as things became a little rough."

"Calm down, Norman my old son. Nobody's packing it in," said Keith Robinson. "We've found the pot of gold, haven't we? Never had such a good time, personally."

He alone, it seemed, had not been turned into a zombie, so tired were we all when we broke up. I noticed that he was the only one of the "musketeers" who seemed impatient to get to whatever venue they had chosen for that morning's wild night.

I did not sleep well, and when eventually my brain stopped racing with scenes from the casino the noises from the early morning traffic kept me awake. Pauline brought me breakfast in bed at ten before she went shopping. I was taking my first weary bite of bacon when the phone rang. It was Blake.

"I must see you urgently," he said.

"What's wrong?"

"I can't discuss it on the phone. Could you come round here?"

"I suppose so. I'll be there at eleven."

Pauline came back a few minutes later. She looked agitated.

"There were two men following me!"

"Are you sure? What kind of men?"

"They were French, well dressed, in their thirties. I'm frightened, Norman."

"I think Blake's had a fright as well by the sound of it. I'm going round to his place. I think you should stay here today. I'll ring you every so often to make sure that you're all right."

I started out for Blake's hotel by a back street.

Passing a pharmacy, I remembered that Pauline had asked me to buy some soap. As I stood at the counter I looked in the mirror and saw two men staring at me. They fitted Pauline's description. I bought the soap and then went to the telephone to call a taxi.

I waited in there until the Citroen cab pulled up outside. I walked fairly quickly out of the shop, got in and gave the driver a fictitious address in a street near Blake's hotel. By the time this had happened, it was too late for the two men to follow in their own car, presumably parked in the vicinity of my hotel.

I paid off the taxi and walked to Blake's hotel. He was alone in his suite.

"Mr. Leigh," he said, "sorry to bother you, but I thought you'd want to know. Strange thing—this phone rang twenty or thirty times between six and nine this morning. Each time I picked it up there was a weird clicking noise at the other end, but nobody spoke."

"Fault in the line probably."

"That isn't all. Ever since about half-past eight this place has been watched. I saw them from the window, three or four of them standing at the corner down there. They kept walking up and down, maybe waiting for somebody to come out."

"Pauline was followed when she went out this morning. I didn't fully believe her until the same couple came after me. I gave them the slip."

"But why on earth do they want to follow us?"

"If they're going to make any moves against us, they'll want to make sure they know where we all are."

"You think then they are planning something?"

"I would say it's a distinct possibility. Could you ring for a taxi? I'll meet you at the café as usual."

"Where are you going?"

"Nowhere in particular. Maybe give them a run for their money."

"You sound as if you're enjoying all this. I'm bloody sure I'm not."

"This is what it was all for—didn't I tell you?"

"I don't understand. We came here to see if your system could work."

"The system? I never had the slightest doubt it would work. I wanted to see what happened when it did. Taking them for a lot of money wouldn't be satisfying unless we caused a bit of a furore, would it?"

"I don't believe it! You wanted to provoke them all the time?"

"Not necessarily. I wanted to take this thing to the limit and see what they would do when they knew we had them beaten."

Startled, Blake nevertheless phoned for a taxi. It came five minutes later.

As we pulled away from the curb two black Simcas came out from a line of parked cars and started to follow us. I had given the driver the name of our hotel but changed my mind and told him instead to take me to the municipal gardens. The incessant phone calls Blake had been getting sounded like psychological warfare; now I'd give them a taste of their own medicine, and wipe the smiles off their faces.

15

As I was paying my taxi driver I saw the two black Simcas pull into the side some twenty yards farther along the pavement. We were outside the municipal gardens. I strolled back along the pavement, reaching into my breast pocket for one of my business cards.

The driver of the first Simca was sitting with the window open, heavily intent on not looking at me. I scribbled the address of our hotel on the back of the card.

Coming up to the car, I threw the card into his lap and said casually: "Why don't you contact me at that address? All this cops-and-robbers stuff is a waste of the taxpayers' money."

My French may not be perfect, but he understood well enough. The expression on his face was a joy to behold.

It was then midday. I strolled over to a café and ordered a dry martini. Within a couple of minutes two men strolled past on the other side of the street, eyeing me intently. They walked on a few yards, turned, came back and then stood against the railings of the municipal gardens. As sleuths they were either rank amateurs or, more likely, they wanted me to see them. I found myself laughing.

I finished my drink and waved at a passing cab, telling

the driver to take me to the local museum. Sure enough, the two black Simcas pulled away from the curb.

Alighting at the museum, I walked slowly up a flight of stairs to where a fair was being held on a high piece of ground. This was thirsty work. I had a lager at one of the stalls. There was no sight of my tail.

At 12:30 P.M. I went back down the hill, caught another cab and told the driver to take me to the promenade. Failing to see anyone following me, I walked into a small public garden and sat on a bench under a palm tree. The faint buzzing of insects and the murmur of the traffic had a relaxing effect. I began to drowse. Then I heard footsteps on the gravel path.

This time it was the two youngish men who had picked me up at the pharmacy. I saw them coming round the angle of the path before they saw me. I sat exactly where I was and stared at them openly.

As soon as they saw me they hesitated, then turned off along a side path. This seemed to indicate that they were, in fact, incompetent rather than deliberately menacing. I found myself laughing again.

At one, I decided to walk slowly to the Café Massena. It was extremely hot, and the glare of sunlight reflected off predominantly white buildings was giving me a headache, so much so I had to sit down on another bench. For a moment I thought I was going to faint.

Knowing I had to get out of the sun, I more or less staggered as far as a small café in the nearest side-street. I ordered a grenadine. My pursuers were not in evidence. I recovered enough to set out walking again. I reached the Massena at 1:25 P.M. and went inside to have another grenadine in the shade.

At 1:30 Mrs. Harper-Biggs and Mrs. Heppenstall arrived. I waved for them to come inside. I called Pauline at the hotel, but she had nothing dramatic to report. A

few minutes later I saw Sherlock and Hopplewell taking seats at one of the outside tables.

"Let's take our drinks outside," said Lettice. "It's a pity to waste the sunshine."

We went outside. Hopplewell ordered a coffee! When Sherlock made some sarcastic remark he replied, apparently by way of explanation, "This place has done wonders for the old chest. I'm thinking of moving here permanently." Blake arrived, followed shortly afterwards by Emma Richardson, Terry Baker and his wife, and Keith Robinson. For ten minutes or so we talked about the weather. Maurice Nathan and George Milton arrived, followed a few minutes later by Peter Vincent and then Fredericks. By two o'clock all twelve of the team were there. I said nothing about my morning chase. Suddenly Lyn Baker blurted out that she and Terry thought they had been followed when they went out to buy baby food that morning.

"We're all getting a little edgy," Blake said sympathetically.

"I say we ought to go home before something happens," Lyn Baker exclaimed, sounding genuinely frightened.

"We're seeing this through no matter what," Terry said sharply.

"I think we should go home!"

Baker raised his voice, "You aren't a member of the team so don't interfere!"

"I've got as much right as anyone else to give my opinion."

"Why don't you shut up?" Baker shouted.

"Shut up yourself!"

By this time we were the center of attraction for everyone else in the café. "Come, come now," said Blake. "Let's not give them the satisfaction of seeing us squabbling among ourselves."

The Bakers glared at each other.

"Why don't we go to the cocktail lounge of the hotel round the corner?" I said. "We can get a bit more privacy there."

We entered the cocktail bar in a group and ordered a variety of drinks. Nobody had much to say. Even Vincent was looking fairly serious. Terry Baker came back from seeing his wife into a taxi. He smiled at me. I called Pauline at the hotel. She seemed quite relaxed. Back at the bar Keith Robinson was telling jokes. "What do you think will happen?" Terry Baker asked me. I shrugged. "As soon as we've finished these drinks we go across to the casino and find out."

"I've told Lyn she's got to go back home. The heat's too much for the baby."

"I think that's sensible."

"Yeah well, we all learn in time, I suppose. Tell you something, I've done all the roistering I need for one lifetime, from now on I save every bloody franc I get my hands on. God, I feel terrible."

"Good. Right then, ladies and gentlemen, time to go to work."

At 2:40 P.M. we crossed the square towards the dull ochre building. Blake walked beside me. He murmured something about having put the cash book in a safe place. "If the authorities got their hands on it they would know exactly how much we had won; it could lead to awkward questions about where the money went."

"You're right, of course. Actually all we have to say is that we spent it. Champagne and wild women."

"In Baker's case all too true, probably. Not to mention Sherlock and Robinson."

"At least they'll have had an experience to talk about when they are old men."

"All you and I have had is hard work."

"I wouldn't say that."

"No?"

"We have proved it can be done—that's something, isn't it? We've made history of a sort, no matter what happens now."

"Not the kind of history one would write to *The Times* about."

"You're not ashamed of all this, are you?"

He made no reply.

The casino doors were still locked at 2:45 when we reached the first-floor landing. We stood there waiting for the commissariat desk to give the order to open them. Most of the faces were apprehensive. "Remember what Mr. Blake said on our first day?" I said cheerfully. "One doesn't make history biting one's nails?"

"I don't have any nails left to bite," said Maurice Nathan.

Three P.M. The doors opened. As we entered the salon M. le Chef de Casino was standing a few feet from the doorway, flanked by some of his minions, smiling sardonically at us.

The first shift took up their positions at our usual table. At 3:03 by the salon clock the tourneur made the first spin of the day. "Thank God they all got seats," said Blake.

"What's wrong with Hopplewell?" I asked.

"He wants to speak to you, I think."

I moved round the table. Hopplewell had a small accumulation of chips in front of him. After some twenty spins his line was 27, 44, 71, bringing his next stake to 98 francs. "What's wrong?" I asked him.

"I'm going to faint," he groaned. "I need a drink."

"I'll take your place." By this time the salon was filling up. We waited until everybody round the table was watching to see where the ball would land. I tapped him on the

shoulder. He moved quickly off the chair to his right and I slipped into it from the left. Black came up on that spin and the croupier shoved chips worth 98 francs against his stake. I put on a stake of 125 francs: a 100-franc plaque and a 25-franc plaque. This won. My line became 27, 44, 71, 98, 125. My next stake was 152 francs. This won. My line became 27, 44, 71, 98, 125, 152. I lost my next two stakes and my line was down to two figures, 71 and 98, giving me a stake of 169 francs.

Then black came into predominance with a vengeance. It came up seven times in a row (ten consecutive wins was the most we saw in all our time at the Casino Municipale). My stakes reached the 600-franc mark.

It looked like being one of the fastest progressions we had experienced.

Then I looked up to see the Chef de Casino staring at me. I smiled gaily at him.

His face tightened.

Then he stepped back from the table and shouted, "*Cessez les jeux!*"

A great silence fell on the salon.

Everybody in the salon waited to hear what the big boss would say next. He said nothing. Then a number of men appeared at our table. Ignoring the other players, they asked the six of us for our admission cards.

We brought them out of our pockets. Maurice Nathan had his snatched from his hand when the two men standing over him thought he was prevaricating. The Chef de Casino approached the table and made a short speech in French.

"Ladies and gentlemen, for reasons I cannot enter into at the moment this casino will now be closed until further notice. As for you, Mesdames Harper-Biggs, Richardson

and Heppenstall, and Messieurs Nathan, Milton and Leigh"—his eyes met mine briefly—"you will all consider yourselves under restraint. You will remain here until the gendarmerie are called."

Any light-headedness I might have been suffering from quickly disappeared. I rose from my chair.

"Monsieur le Chef," I said calmly, "you will recall the undertaking you gave us only a few days ago, that we would suffer no obstacle to playing a system against the table? What has happened to change your mind?"

"Shut up!" he barked. I was amazed. All round me faces were registering shock at this scandalous outbreak.

"I will not shut up," I said. "Am I to understand that we are not to leave this casino?"

"Yes!"

"Then I demand that I be allowed to contact the British Consulate."

"You may use the telephone at the desk—and remember to pay for the call!"

None of the desk staff would give me the number of the British Consulate. I thumbed through the Nice directory until I found the entry, *Conseil Britannique*.

When I got through, an arrogant voice told me the consul was too busy to speak to me.

"My name is Leigh," I said. "I am with some friends in the Casino Municipale. We are all British citizens and we are being held here under unlawful restraint. They refuse to let us leave the salon. Does that sound less important than whatever else the consul is doing?"

There was a good deal of humming and hawing. I was told that somebody would come over to the casino as soon as circumstances permitted.

"In that case will you kindly give me the number of the British Embassy in Paris?"

"There is no need to make such a fuss—"

I put the receiver down on him and dialled enquiries. I got through to the Embassy in Paris after about ten minutes and explained the situation to the official who took my call. He promised to take immediate action.

I went back into the main part of the salon. Our group was being questioned by the men who had demanded their admission cards. "Say nothing to these people until the consul gets here," I told everybody.

By the time the man from the Consulate turned up the salon was empty save for the thirteen of us and the staff of the casino. Her Majesty's delegate was a weedy man in his fifties, apparently out of his depth in this situation.

However, he was the best we were going to get, so I gave him a brief résumé of what had happened. "You can see we are being physically restrained from leaving this casino. We have committed no crime—indeed, these people have not even made any allegations against us."

"I'm sure it's all a misunderstanding," he burbled. His ineffectuality exasperated me. "If the gendarmerie is not here within a couple of minutes," I announced, "we will walk out. Let them try to stop us by force if they like. We'll see then what kind of scandal you have on your hands, Monsieur le Chef."

"Come come, let's be reasonable," said the man from the Consulate.

I snarled: "Be reasonable? Why don't you give *them* that advice? We have done nothing except play roulette. And win, of course."

A smallish man detached himself from the group who had taken our admission cards. "We would like to know what you and your friends have done with the money you won from this casino—you realize there are

restrictions on the amount of French currency that can be sent out of France?"

I handed him my notepad. "Will you put your questions in writing and sign the page? Here is my pen if you don't have one."

He grimaced and then turned his back on me. I burst out laughing. The Consulate official frowned at me to keep quiet.

"Keep quiet yourself, sir," I snapped at him, ready now to explode. "What the hell have you done to help us anyway? If the police are not here forthwith we go out through that door—fighting if necessary."

The idea of Cynthia Harper-Biggs and Lettice Heppenstall battling against the phalanx of men surrounding us made me laugh out loud as soon as I had finished this tirade. No doubt I was a little out of control.

That was when five or six uniformed gendarmes came into the casino. One of them brought out a notebook.

"When I call your name please answer," he said. He started reading from his list. We all answered correctly.

"I wish you to come with us if you please," said the senior policeman.

"Where to?" Blake demanded.

"The headquarters of the Police des Jeux."

"Do we go?" Blake asked me.

"We must—don't give them any excuse for accusing us of failing to co-operate with the law."

The Chef de Casino and his minions impassively watched us go through the swing doors with the gendarmes. Nothing was said.

We came out into the blinding sunshine. It was 5:30 P.M. We started off walking through the town behind the gendarmes.

"Funny way of arresting us," said Keith Robinson. "Follow-my-leader to jail?"

I looked back. There was not a single policeman behind us.

"I don't think these chaps consider we've broken the law," Blake said.

"We could just run for it then," Keith said.

"Then we *would* be in trouble," I told him. "Let's just wait and see what they have planned for us."

After ten minutes' meandering through the back streets we came to a dilapidated blue building with white louver shutters.

We were led in through the main entrance. Our police escort, who had hardly bothered to look back once during our progress through the town, went down a passageway, stopping at the door of a large, sparsely furnished room with a long table under a window high in the wall.

Seated behind the table were five high-ranking police officers. The heat in the room was terrific.

One of them started to read out a list of our names. Each of us answered in turn. We were then told to sit down, a strange invitation as there were thirteen of us and only two shaky cane chairs. Mrs. Harper-Biggs and Mrs. Heppenstall lowered themselves into them gingerly. The officer who had read out our names sat down and another stood up.

"Ladies and gentlemen," he said in passable English, "I wish to assure you that you have done nothing criminal and you have not broken the casino regulations—as far as we of the Police des Jeux are concerned you are honourable men and ladies. However, and without assigning any reason, we have to inform you that you are hereby banned for life from playing roulette in the Casino Municipale."

I started to say something, but he waved me down. "I cannot enter into discussions with you; it is pointless to put any questions to me. I would warn all of you that if you should make any attempt to regain admission to

the Casino Municipale that will constitute a criminal offense. That is all I have to say to you. You may go now. Good day."

The great coup was over. We were shown out into the sunshine. Dazed and bewildered, our little party hesitated on the pavement. "What do we do now then?" asked Keith Robinson.

"I think we should all go back to my place for a drink," said Blake. "It looks as if our little venture has come to an end."

"I don't see why," Terry Baker said aggressively. "Plenty more casinos, aren't there?"

"I should imagine we're banned from all of them," said Blake. "I can make enquiries, if you like."

"Of course we *could* go to the Salle Privée, Monte Carlo," I said, looking at Baker. "How are you off for capital?"

"Need you bloody well ask?" Baker retorted.

We decided to wait while Blake attempted to discover whether we had been banned from all the municipal casinos and meet the following day as usual at the Café Massena. When we did so, Blake said he had been on the phone all morning. "We've been banned by the French Ministry of the Interior. These municipal casinos are administered centrally from Enghien les Bains, and if you are banned from one of them, you are automatically banned in all the others."

"There are other casinos, private ones," said Sherlock.

"Go through all that again?" said Maurice Nathan.

We were having an inconclusive discussion, only Baker and Sherlock apparently having the stomach for starting the whole process again, when I noticed three or four men watching us from the other side of the square. I nudged George Milton. The others turned to see what

we were looking at. One of the group, a tall thin man in a dark suit, came across the square towards us, walking deliberately, without haste.

He came up to the three tables we had pushed together and looked at us all in turn.

"When are you leaving for England?" he said finally, in good English.

"What concern is it of yours?" I asked. "Are you from the police? If so, may I see your credentials?"

He gave me a long look, shaking his head. "I think it will be better for all of you to leave here quickly," he said. Then he walked back across the square. His associates stood there listening to him and watching us.

That did it.

We had a dinner party that night in Mrs. Harper-Biggs' hotel. After a few drinks Blake let himself go as far as to recite by heart Kipling's poem "If." Released from the tension of the past few days, we all became fairly jolly. I contented myself with a short speech of thanks to all of them for the magnificent way they had worked together.

"We've all come a long way from my roulette academy in Twickenham," I said. "We don't need any histrionics, we know what we've proved. We made the system work, we won a lot of money, we were so successful we made a government nervous—above all I think I can truthfully say we have all shared an experience we won't easily forget. I don't know if we'll ever meet again, but before we break up I should very much like to thank each and every one of you for having faith enough in me to take part. I give you a toast: to our gallant band of thirteen."

postscript

What did it all prove?

At the time I was satisfied merely to think that all those years, all those disasters and farces, finally produced an undeniable triumph. The thirteen of us made gaming history in proving that a determined group of people working to a scientific system can beat the casino on its own terms. In our eight days at the Casino Municipale our winnings came to about 800,000 francs—£58,000 ($163,000).

I kept up contact with some of the twelve over the next few years, although our general mood was against annual reunions and the like—we had done it together and there was no need to surround our memories with ritual celebrations. Mrs. Harper-Biggs and Mrs. Heppenstall had become close friends on the trip and remained so. Blake married the girl he'd been engaged to before we went to France. Sydney Hopplewell, who told Pauline at that last night's dinner party that he had never known such good friends, eased up on his drinking. Each of the team made about £4,230 (approximately $11,844) in the eight days we actually played in the Casino Municipale, but even tax-free it was hardly enough to change the whole course of their lives.

It is very likely that Terry Baker's life was changed for the worse. It seemed probable that he and his wife would split up. How much of the money he and Sherlock and Robinson managed to salvage from their headlong adoption of riotous living I prefer not to conjecture. I know that Maurice Nathan kept most of his winnings and set himself up in business again. What happened to Thomas Fredericks I don't know, although I'm fairly sure he was not going back to polish a humble office chair, not wearing the kind of suits he took home from the Riviera.

Peter Vincent got fairly drunk on that last night and made some sort of pass at Emma Richardson, who turned him down, needless to say.

As for myself—Pauline and I separated and were finally divorced. I would not blame it entirely on my obsession with roulette.

One thing I can say with some certainty, however. I proved my point and I had the supreme satisfaction of doing it before the eyes of the man who had found my father's bankruptcy so amusing all those years before. Yet by the time we had become so successful that we had to be marched out of the casino and banned for life by the French government I had lost any lurking desire to flaunt my triumph in his face. Winning is the cure for a gambling obsession. I remember something Peter Vincent said one night in the casino. The usual mocking smile about his eyes, he surveyed the crowded tables and remarked, "Amazing to what lengths we higher primates will go for a bit of amusement, isn't it?"

That seemed to put roulette in perspective. Having achieved the goal which had ruled most of my adult years, I found life strangely empty. A cured addiction leaves a very large void. One would like to think that the years bring maturity—looking back, I can only conclude that there are no half-measures with an obsessive

personality. I have always had a bee in my bonnet about the way Authority loads the dice in its own favour and I daresay my life would have been more fruitful if I had been content to knuckle down to the preordained order of things.

However—I did make a little bit of history.

Do you wonder *now* why a man who discovered the "perfect system" for beating the wheel could regard roulette as something of which he had, finally, been *cured*?

And yet . . . is an addict ever really cured?

When news of this book began to spread I was approached by an American who wanted to know if my system would work in Las Vegas.

I explained the difference between the French and the American wheel. The latter has thirty-eight compartments and two zeros. The double zero gives the bank an advantage of 5.26 percent—an additional feature being that on the double-zero wheel the bet *cannot* be halved (*partager*) if zero appears, neither can it be left on the table "imprisoned" (*en prison*), to have its fate decided by the next spin. On the American wheel all bets are lost when zero comes up.

How would this affect the Reverse Labouchère? The additional advantage would probably make the difference between winning say $2,500 (single-zero wheel) and $2,350 (double-zero wheel) in a day. This would hardly worry the serious player—but there is another complication.

The spin of the American wheel in a Las Vegas casino is governed purely by time. The croupiers do not wait for players to place their stakes. On a French wheel you will have approximately thirty spins to the hour—the American wheel will be spun sixty to sixty-five times in the same period.

This is a minor disadvantage—the player has less time

for calculations between spins. Yet once the brain can cope, this faster rate becomes a positive advantage. The team would require twice as much capital but it should show slightly more than *double the profits*, simply because there are more spins to work on.

"Well, what's stopping us forming a syndicate to have a crack at one of the casinos in Vegas?" this American asked.

"No!" was my immediate reaction. "I'm finished with roulette."

"All that money waiting to be won, but you're not interested? Are you sure?"

I tried to make a joke about it. "After all, does one wish to climb Everest *twice?*"

"Really?" he said sarcastically. "Sure you aren't frightened your win in Nice wasn't just a fluke?"

I was so annoyed I could hardly speak. I had *proved* that my theory worked. I did not have to go on and on proving it, did I? We had made *history*, damn the man.

And yet, the more I think about it, the more I hear myself asking:

Why not?